The Book of David: My East Harlem Love Story

Betty Winston Bayé

ROYSTON Publishing

BK Royston Publishing
P. O. Box 4321
Jeffersonville, IN 47131
502-802-5385 | http://www.bkroystonpublishing.com

© Copyright – 2019

All Rights Reserved. No part of this book may be reproduced, stored in a retrieval system, or transmitted by any means without the written permission of the author.

Cover Design: Derrick J. Thomas

Cover Layout: Elite Covers Gad Savage

Back Cover Photo Credit: Jessica Ebelhar

ISBN-13: 978-1-946111-78-4

LCCN: 2019907821

Printed in the United States of America

To Our Parents
Thank you for Life and Love
Rest in Peace

"Love is like a virus. It can happen to anybody at any time."

Maya Angelou

Contents

Dedication — iii

Prologue — ix

Chapter 1 — 1
Closer to Heaven - (Phil Perry)

Chapter 2 — 9
Hello Stranger - (Barbara Lewis)

Chapter 3 — 29
Apaga la luz - (La India)

Chapter 4 — 37
You Ought to Be with Me - (Al Green)

Chapter 5 — 53
I Blame You - (Ledisi)

Chapter 6 — 59
Ain't No Stoppin' Us Now - (McFadden & Whitehead)

Chapter 7 — 65
Living Just Enough for the City - (Stevie Wonder)

Chapter 8 — 71
Over the Rainbow - (Patti LaBelle)

Chapter 9 — 89
Insanity - (Gregory Porter & Lalah Hathaway)

Chapter 10 — 93
Feel the Fire - (Peabo Bryson)

Chapter 11 — 101
Slow Blues - (John Coltrane)

Chapter 12 — 109
Everything Must Change - (Oleta Adams)

Part 2: The Journey — 133
A quote from Kahlil Gibran

Chapter 13 — 135
The Long and Winding Road - (The Beatles)

Chapter 14 — 143
You're All I Need to Get By -
(Marvin Gaye & Tammi Terrell)

Chapter 15 — 153
Joy and Pain - (Frankie Beverly & Maze)

Chapter 16 — 161
Angel of Love - (Michel Colombier with Phil Perry)

Chapter 17 — 169
Georgia on My Mind - (Ray Charles)

Chapter 18 — 215
Miss You - (Etta James)

Acknowledgements — 223

Author's Bio — 225

Prologue

Storytellers use various means to draw readers in and to encourage them to want stay awhile. My writing device for this memoir was to use songs as my chapter titles along with the names of the artists who perform my favorite versions. All the songs mentioned as chapter titles and within the manuscript in one way or the other were the hooks that helped me to recall the girl that I was and the woman that I'm still becoming.

When I very young, my godmother, "Annie," aka Sarah Theola Pinder, bought me a Mickey Mouse record player for Christmas. It was intended to play the children's songs on the brightly colored discs that came with the record player. But my record player was pressed into service whenever the grown folks' record player was on the fritz. My parents, uncles, aunts and their friends partied to the music of Johnny Ace, Ruth Brown, LaVerne Baker, Brook Benton, Dinah Washington, Fats Domino, Sam Cooke to name a few. I loved watching them have a good time. Nearly all of them had migrated to New York City from their segregated hometowns. Most of them had little formal education and held down menial jobs which earned them very little money or respect but when the stylus dug down into the grooves of their favorite vinyl recordings, they were kings and queens.

When I was older, I saved up my money to buy a "portable" record player. It was big and heavy and came in three pieces - the dropdown turntable and two detachable speakers. I would sit that contraption on the window sill of the tiny bedroom that I shared with my two younger sisters and blast my music. I played The Shirelles, The Chantels, The Skyliners, The Jive Five, Little Anthony and the Imperials, Frankie Lyman and the Teenagers and the Bobbettes, whose members also lived in East Harlem. Early Motown music was also on my playlist. I loved Mary Wells, The Miracles, The Temptations and Gladys Knight and the Pips.

David and I grew up on doo wop, R&B and Latin music. When he was dying, I sat by his hospice bed and played music that gave me solace and that I hoped would comfort my sweetheart as he journeyed to his death.

The Book of David: My East Harlem Love Story

Chapter 1

Closer to Heaven - (Phil Perry)

I arrived at Our Lady of Perpetual Help Home extra early. I wanted to get to the hospice in downtown Atlanta to check on my sweetheart before setting out on my seven-hour drive to Louisville, Kentucky. I had been away from my home there for more than two months and was going back to prepare the keynote address I was to deliver in Danville, Kentucky, at Centre College's Martin Luther King Jr. Day program. It was a longstanding commitment.

I had never been to Our Lady before visiting hours, and that Saturday I observed the morning routines at the hospice to which David had been admitted the day before Thanksgiving. Sister Damien, Our Lady's chief administrator, delivered a sweet morning prayer over the loudspeaker. After a short while, a priest and several of the nuns of the Dominican Sisters of Hawthorne who lived on-site went from room to room, patient to patient, offering sacraments to all who were able and wished to partake. Not being Catholic, I didn't understand all the rituals, but the sacredness of greeting the new day with prayer and Thanksgiving was not lost on me. David was restless and agitated, nevertheless. I let the safety rail down on his bed and moved in to comfort him. I patted my baby's haggard and still handsome face. I kissed him, laid my head on his chest and listened to his heart beat.

"I love you, Moodles. I'll be back before you know it," I whispered, using the nickname I called him. He called me "Moo," or "Moo Moo," but I don't recall how we came to use these names for each other. I fiddled with his sheets and tried to fluff his pillow. David's head was heavy. At that stage of his cancer journey, David rarely spoke, and when he did, what came out were fragmented sentences and seemingly random thoughts. David's eyes popped open one day, for example, and he looked around his hospice room, then at me, and asked, "Whose house is this? It's not my house?"

On another occasion, he said, "They're opening the gates." When I asked who is opening the gates, David never answered. He closed his eyes and fell back to sleep. Was he recollecting the massive wrought-iron gates at Our Lady that he passed through in the ambulance that transported him from the WellStar Tranquility

Hospice in Austell? Was he seeing the biblical Pearly Gates? I cherished David's utterances, looking for hidden meanings, and wrote them in my journal that has theologian Reinhold Niebuhr's "Serenity Prayer" on the front cover: "God, grant me the serenity to accept the things I cannot change, courage to change the things I can, and wisdom to know the difference."

While David didn't speak much, his hearing was acute during the final weeks of his life. I could tell that by his facial expressions and reactions, even when his eyes were closed. When conversations were being had around him, he would frown, cock his head to the side, and sometimes laugh or smile. Mostly though, David slept or appeared to be asleep. On that Saturday morning, January 17, 2015, David was wide awake. He followed me with his eyes and without warning reached out and punched me in my side. The force of his jab caught me off guard, and it hurt. Where was his strength coming from? It wasn't there yesterday, the day before or the day before that.

David's hard thrusts persisted. Were his left-handed pokes mere reflexes? I wondered. David's right side had become paralyzed a few weeks earlier, and the funny thing is, he seemed not to notice that his right arm and good hand no longer worked. As if to compensate, his left arm and hand seemed to develop minds of their own. David would lift that hand, and it would hang suspended mid-air for unnaturally long periods of time. It was as if David was a marionette and an invisible puppeteer was pulling his strings.

What was David trying to communicate with his jabs to my ribs? Was he saying scat, scram, go? Get out of my sight? Or was he wordlessly screaming my name or his nickname for me, "Betty, Moo Moo, look at me! Are you blind? Can't you see that I'm dying right now? Can't you see? Do you not understand that this battle is almost over? Don't you realize that I won't be here when you get back Tuesday? Can't you see? Can't you sense that this is our last time together — that this is the last time you'll lay eyes on me in this place and in this sorry condition?"

Of course, I was aware that the sand in the hourglass of David's life was running low, but if I had any notion that he would be dead in a few hours, I never would have left him. We had been through so much together.

My last morning with David is a scene that plays over and over in my head, and each new showing brings fresh tears and new insights. At times, I am consumed with guilt for not realizing that I was leaving David to die, so I could go home to Kentucky to write a speech.

I had been with him every step of his cancer journey, and there was nothing heroic about it. Whatever I did was because I loved him and because in my heart, I believed God was trying to teach me something. He wanted to show a childless woman what it means to take care of someone who is suffering terribly and is as helpless as a baby. David would have done the same for me, so being there with him, for him, was the least that I could do.

David was a child of God, and his death that afternoon caught his caretakers by surprise. I got the news in a telephone call from his son just after I got home in Louisville. When I returned to Our Lady about a week later to thank the nuns and the staff for their compassion and excellent care of David, they said that his death that day was unexpected. In fact, David was more animated and engaged than he had been in some time. He was awake, they said, and he actually drank a little Boost nutritional supplement for lunch. In his final weeks, David often resisted anyone's attempts to feed him. He would clamp his mouth shut so tightly that not even a tiny straw could penetrate past his lips.

Everyone's back was turned when he slipped away, quietly, the caretakers said. That was so David and so the opposite of the unnerving death rattles of the man in the bed next to his. It went on for hours, and then came the awful silence. I never saw his face because his curtains were always drawn. I'm told the man had been at Our Lady for months, That's the policy. Once you're in, you stay until you die, for as long as it takes. David's quiet exit was also unlike another of his roommates, who as death closed in howled, "Mama, Mama! I'm sorry, Mama. I'm sorry."

I had been with David for almost all the 568 days from the stage IIIB lung cancer diagnosis in June 2013 to his death. Yet I wasn't with him when he died at 2:25 in the afternoon, only hours after I had left him.

I will forever ponder whether David's jabs to my ribs were his final, conscious act of trying to protect me from what he knew was coming sooner rather than later. I can believe that he had little confidence that I could handle his dying in my presence. One of David's endearing characteristics, in fact, is that from the moment we committed to one another, he was my protector. He would stand back and watch others watching me. In many photographs, he's standing just over my shoulder. He took pains to assure me that, come what may, he had my back.

When I faced hard choices, was the object of harsh criticism, or was betrayed by someone I thought was a friend, David would sweep me into his arms, press my face into his big, wide chest, lean down and whisper, "I got you, baby." I loved him for that. David was a man's man. He was big, handsome and strong. So yes, I can imagine him negotiating with God.

"God, Betty's been here for me, and I know she loves me, and you know that she loves me. I don't want to leave her, but God, you know and I know that I've got to get up out of here. God, can you fix it so that the last sounds I hear on this earth won't be her crying, screaming and begging me back from my destiny. You understand what I'm saying, God? So, may I make a suggestion? Send her away. I'm not afraid to die, but I know that she's afraid for me."

Yeah, I can imagine David saying something like that.

Thirty-one years before David died, I chose the "Serenity Prayer" for the palm cards that I ordered for the funeral of the first man that I ever loved, George Washington Winston, my daddy. Lung and throat cancer claimed his life, too, as well that of my mother, Betty Jane Brown Winston.

Cancer is a demon out of hell.

Sitting with David for hours gave me time to think deeply and to write in my journal with great intentionality. I wrote so that when David was gone and my own recollections grew foggy, I could open my journal and remember who called, who visited, and who prayed with us and for us. I could open my journal and reconstruct how David looked when he laughed, when he was sad, and when he was being ultra-demanding.

I've given most of David's clothes away but kept a couple of his favorite T-shirts. Whenever I slip them on, I feel like a naughty girl because David didn't like me to wear his tees. He didn't want "titty bumps" in his shirts. That's ridiculous, but that's how he felt. I don't think he would mind, however, that I've kept his favorite white straw "Steve Harvey" fedora. Once, David plopped his hat on the head of my beautiful brass bust from Benin. I was peeved and reminded him that the bust was a work of art of incalculable value. No matter, I came home one day to find that David had adorned the bust with both the hat and sunglasses, for goodness sakes! I couldn't be angry. After David died, his fedora got a permanent home atop the bust in the living room.

It's interesting, at least to me, how the most trivial things trigger my memories of David, such as when I walk down the cookie aisle of a grocery store and see boxes of Oreos and Chips Ahoy. David, a diabetic, was passionate about his cookies and Hostess' cream-filled chocolate cupcakes.

David's son, also named David, aka Levet, his middle name and the maiden name of his paternal great grandmother, arrived at Our Lady shortly after his father had died. "My dad actually seemed to be smiling," he said when he called to tell me the news. "He was at peace. All the stress was gone from his face."

I envy Levet that glimpse, and it's likely that he envies me for having been the last of the loved ones to see his father still breathing.

About two weeks before David's passing, I requested that his bed be moved next to the big picture window in his room. Though David's attendants had no problem doing so, I felt motivated to tell them why.

"David was a child of the sun," I said. "He's a proud Nuyorican. That's a Puerto Rican born and raised in New York City."

I wanted David's bed by the window so that he could look out and see the sun, the clouds, and when it rained, watch the beads of water slide down the glass and puddle at the bottom. My prayer was that David, even in his weakened state, would look through that window and marvel at God's power as it manifested in a rainbow. I wanted the man I loved to feel the sun as it warmed and kissed his brown skin. I wanted David, with whatever consciousness he still had left, to feel alive and to partake of God's grace in the external world and the world inside of him.

I also told the attendants that he loved to brew Café Bustelo in the mornings, and that he really could "throw down" in the kitchen. He learned to cook watching and helping his mother, Dona Lydia.

I shared that the first big disagreement David and I had was food-related He wanted us was take our meals at the dining room table, which seemed to me, too much fuss for just two people. So, we compromised. We could save the dining room for special meals, but at other times, we could eat at the kitchen counter or on snack trays in the den.

"One day, I got so annoyed by David's insistence on formal dining," I told the attendants, "that I stormed out of the house, jumped in my car and drove around aimlessly for a couple hours talking to myself. Who was David to insist that we eat together as if we were a big family? It was ridiculous. I even questioned whether I had made a mistake to invite David to leave Pittsburgh to come live with me in Kentucky."

I'm not sure why I shared that particular incident. I guess I wanted those who were caring for David to get a sense of his humanity and a sense of the man he was before they encountered him, mostly silent, unable to walk and with a mind and body savaged by cancer.

"David loved to play chess, fish and to swim," I explained. "He was a huge fan of Animal Planet and the History Channel, and he devoured every issue of the *National Geographic* magazines that came in the mail."

I told the attendants that David loved salsa, jazz, R&B, African chanting and drum music. He said he had been initiated into Santeria at some point in his adulthood. The religion, which is predicated on the beliefs of the Yoruba people of Africa, spread to the Caribbean islands, including Puerto Rico. It incorporates elements of Catholicism, and many who practice Santeria remain members of the Catholic church and refer to its saints by Yoruba names.

Unlike me, David was not a chatterbox by nature. He could sit quiet for hours. He meditated without making a big deal of it, and he found immense pleasure in nature. David, for all his worldliness, was deeply spiritual. He didn't brag about it or seek to explain it; he just was.

I soothed myself with my imaginings that when death showed up, David greeted it as a friend who had come to take him to his real home.

In my imagination, David stepped out of his mortal, rotting body and walked right through that big glass window. I imagined him glancing back a time or two and then heading straight toward the sun. David walked, something he hadn't been able to do in quite some time, and then he ran until he disappeared behind the clouds, where awaited his mother, father, brother Michael, sister Felina, nephew Jesus, and his old East Harlem friends Duke, Hop and Dimas.

Chapter 2

Hello Stranger - (Barbara Lewis)

Unlike Bobby Womack's soulful confession in the song, "Lookin' for a Love," I was not seeking that in the summer of 2010, nor had I planned to be in New York the third Saturday in August. Yet, I was standing outside Penn Station, sweating in the intense heat, hailing a cab uptown. It was almost as hot as it had been in Egypt, where I'd been a few weeks earlier. Getting a cab in Manhattan isn't easy in any kind of weather when you're black and when even many black and beige cabbies will pass you up for the white person nearby.

Racism is insidious, but I won't go there.

Anyhow, I was on my way to the annual East River Houses Old Timers' Reunion. East River is the public housing project where I grew up. My sister Debbie Winston Blakes is on the organizing committee, and my other sister, Georgeann Winston Eaddy, had flown up from Atlanta for the reunion. They weren't expecting me. I had already told them I had other plans. I was going to be in D.C. with my friend Vanessa Williams, to do some shopping, eat some crabs, and to celebrate our mutual friend Roy Campbell's 50th birthday at a casino outside Philadelphia. Roy is a former fashion editor at *The Philadelphia Inquirer,* where Vanessa was a reporter before moving on to *The Washington Post.*

The party was fabulous, of course. V and I stayed overnight and stopped by Roy's apartment in Wilmington, Delaware, on our way back to D.C. We were laughing and gossiping about who among Roy's famous friends did or didn't show up for his party. I happened to mention the reunion in New York. What did I do that for? Roy and Vanessa decided that it was ridiculous for me to be that close and not seize the opportunity to go home and spend time with my sisters. Their guilt tripping worked. Next thing I knew, Roy was checking the Amtrak train schedule, and he and V were whisking me to the station in Wilmington. Roy got the ticket, and the two of them practically heaved me onto the train for the two-hour trip.

The Old Timers' Reunion in the "Big Park" at the rear of the housing project was well under way by the time I arrived. I had spent many wonderful days in that park, playing in the sandbox, riding the wooden seesaw, climbing the monkey bars, pumping high on the swings and being a nuisance to the teenagers who claimed the "Big Park" as the place for lovers. The park is also the place where one day many years ago, little Brenda McCullough pumped too high, flew out of a swing and ended up with mouth and facial injuries that required many surgeries over many years.

As soon as I got there, I parked my little red suitcase by the fence. My sisters spied me, ran over and gave me hugs.

"I thought you said you weren't coming," said Debbie, the only member of the Old Timers' organizing committee who still lives in East River. "It's a long story," I said, promising that I would share later.

My mood lightened as I made the rounds of the benches, tables and lawn chairs, stopping every few feet to greet former neighbors, church members and the dwindling number of my mother's friends: Mary Yancey, Mitzy Handy, Olivia Williams, Leola Glover, Emily Coulter, Kathleen Green, Alice Richardson, Carol Wilson and Theresa Stephens. I scanned the make-shift memorial wall made of heavy construction paper that somebody tacked to the chain-link fence and covered with the obituaries of former residents of the East River projects. Among the dozens were the obits of Mom, Dad and Mrs. Sarah Walton, a wonderful woman and great cook who worked with my mother in the kitchen of the East River Houses day-care center.

After a while, I was glad that V and Roy had strongly encouraged me to attend the reunion.

Much about my old hood was still the same, but East Harlem, was changing. White people were back. Many whites lived there when I was a kid, but as their fortunes rose, they exercised their skin privilege and left us behind.

Now, after decades of rarely venturing above 96th Street on foot, white folks were moving back into East Harlem, and the black and brown old timers believed that, just as in central Harlem and the South Bronx, poor folks, and black and browns of modest means will be pushed out.

Gentrification is a mild way of saying "take-over." Unfortunately, many white people's definition of integration is 98 percent them and 2 percent everybody else. Fifty-fifty doesn't seem to work for them. The time may not be far off when all the public housing projects in East Harlem will be bulldozed or re-purposed as so-called mixed-income housing, which to me is euphemism for more whites and fewer everybody else.

It's political. It's financial, and the redeveloping hordes will insist that it's neither racist nor personal.

East River projects, for example, is a short hop to LaGuardia Airport via the Triborough Bridge, aka the Robert F. Kennedy Bridge. The smaller Third Avenue Bridge that connects East Harlem to the South Bronx, the gateway to Westchester County and upstate New York, is only 20 blocks north. The East River Drive, the namesake for the projects where I grew up, is easily accessible to the tawny East Side neighborhoods south of 96th Street. Gracie Mansion, the official mayoral residence, is within walking distance of the East River projects, and the United Nations is a quick taxi or bus ride away.

The East Side has got it going on, and East Harlem, with its river views and convenient public transportation, is ripe for de-population that will in short order be followed by re-population. You can stay if you can pay. Harlem is gentrifying more rapidly, but as of this writing East Harlem is not far behind.

At the reunion, the deejay was doing his thing and some of the old timers were doing the Electric Slide when I spied a man making his way through the park. When he got closer, I heard myself shouting, "David! David Rivera! Oh, my God! Look at you." I reached up and wrapped my arms around his neck. I was truly glad to see my Puerto Rican boy crush in the flesh after decades of him being out of sight and mind.

David broke into a smile of recognition.

"Betty Winston!" he bellowed.

Like a scene straight out of some sappy soap opera, I came down with a case of wobbly knees. The noise of the reunion crowd and the vehicles zipping up and down the East River Drive — *everything* but David Rivera — faded to black.

He had never been to an Old Timers' Reunion, and technically, David wasn't an East River projects old timer. He grew up in the Woodrow Wilson projects, which were newer and separated from East River by 105th Street. Even so, he was an honorary old timer because when we were kids, David hung out, played chess, played basketball and chased girls with the guys from East River.

I first laid eyes on David Rivera in 1960. I was with some girlfriends hanging out on a bench in "the middle" of East River projects when we spied him, a new boy in our hood. I'm sure he knew that we were checking him out, but he pretended not to notice. Eventually, I learned that his name was David and that he lived in the Wilson projects across the street. I quickly developed a mad crush on the stocky, brown-skinned cutie, but it never evolved into an official boyfriend/girlfriend thing. My father didn't play that. I was a totally innocent teenager. I did a little kissing, flirting and "grinding" to slow songs at red-light, blue-light parties in our neighborhood, but whatever sweet nothings some horny, sweaty boy whispered in my ear, I heard George Winston's voice much louder in my other ear. "Don't bring no baby in here. You better finish high school."

I never wanted to disappoint my father or my mother. Though they are long deceased, it's a source of pride that nary a boy that I grew up can honestly claim that he went "all the way" with little Betty Winston.

Even so, I knew that David knew that I had a crush on him. "Wait up. Where you going?" he would ask when he spied me coming out of my building and then he would fall in beside me as I crossed First Avenue on my way to the shops, Mr. B's, Henry's or Choo-Choo's. The shopkeepers didn't require cash on the spot from the regulars; they knew each family by name. They "trusted" us. They would diligently record the bread, milk, cold cuts, cigarettes, beer, soda, candy and so forth in composition notebooks that they kept behind the counter. They expected to get their money when their customers got paid or when their welfare checks came. The honor system worked.

Some stores in our neighborhood, including a popular pizza parlor, were gangster-owned and operated. They were fronts for illegal gambling, and in particular "the numbers" racket. My parents and most of their friends played "the numbers" just about every day. Number runners, who expected to get a cut for their services, would go door-to-door in the tenements and the projects, collecting the players' slips and their bets. When someone hit big, say for $500 or $1,000, they would splurge on new clothes, furniture, appliances or other items they couldn't otherwise afford. The growing popularity of government-run lotteries have cut into the business, but "numbers" still are a lucrative, untaxed underground economy in many poor communities.

What I remember about young David Rivera is that he was big for his age and wasn't goofy and nasty like some of the boys in the projects who laid mirrors on the ground so they could look up girls' dresses or were always snickering about how they had "copped some drawers" (gotten into a girl's panties) or wanted to.

Six decades later, I cannot extract from the cobwebbed corners of my mind exactly when or how I first actually connected with David after seeing him walking through the projects for the first time. Still, I know for sure that I definitely was crushing on the "new boy," and he was crushing on me.

My foggy memories of my relationship with David sent me to the telephone to ask Ronald Richardson, a mutual friend of David and me, whose family had lived in the same building as mine in the projects.

"Ronald, help!" I began our conversation. "Please refresh me on how it worked back in the day when a boy and a girl liked one another." A retired banker, Ronald has lived in the Chicago area for decades. He relished my question and so began a marathon dialogue that veered between hilarious and sad. Ronald is a year older than me, and our April birthdays are two days apart.

"I'm glad you caught me when I can still remember," he said before launching into his recollections of the foolishness we engaged in when we were kids, including "macking out" sessions in the windowless staircases of building 410 in East River projects.

"Everybody had a floor," Ronald said, "we would unscrew the ceiling lights, and we could still hear what was going on above or below us. After a while, you'd hear the girls saying, "Stop! No! Stop! Get off me."

"Was I ever in the staircase?" I asked.

"Yes, you were," Ronald insisted.

My response, "I don't recall," elicited laughter from my old friend. Ronald ran down how he recalled boy/girl relationships worked when we were teenagers.

"There were spoken and unspoken relationships," he said. He used our friends Butch Williams and Judy Mizell as an example of a spoken relationship. "Everybody knew that they were together, and nothing was going to change that," he said. "None of the guys would talk to Judy." Butch and Judy did get married.

The unspoken relationships, according to Ronald, were ones that were "never consummated," not meaning sexually, but just not declared in the way that we declared them "back in the day."

For example, Ronald said, "If we were hanging out on the benches and a guy laid his head in your lap, he was telling the world that you were going together. If a guy walked through the projects holding your hand, he was letting the other fellows know that you were his girl." I do recall that some boys, when they were rejected by a girl they liked, resorting to making fun of her as if insults would win her heart.

We were so silly.

Ronald named young girlfriends of mine in the projects with whom he claimed to have had "unspoken" relationships. "I used to like you," he finally said, "because you were new, but Mickey Williams got to you first. I was dumb." I obviously was dumb as well because it never occurred to me that Ronald was making a play for me when he would lower his homemade "walkie-talkie" (a piece of rope with a tin can with the bottom and top cut out) down to my window. He lived on the third floor, and I lived on the second floor in building 402. Ronald's tin can would bump against our kitchen window, and I would open it and reach out and grab the can, and Ronald would say, "Calling Betty Winston. Calling Betty Winston."

We really thought that we were talking through the cans, when in fact our windows were close enough that we could hear each other without them.

So, based on Ronald's recollections, David and I clearly had an unspoken relationship, and with good reason. My biggest reason was my dad. The other reasons, I imagine looking back, is that David wasn't talkative, and was, unbeknownst to me or our clique, a couple of years younger, though he looked our age. He might also have been a little shy — at least with me. When we reconnected as adults, he said more than once that he thought of me as a smart girl that he didn't want to "mess up."

Ronald's recollections of David, meanwhile, were that, "He was a pretty good athlete. He played softball, basketball and baseball, and he shot craps in the Big Park and smoked reefer like everybody else, but he was kind of goofy and not the kind of guy to let on that he liked a girl.

"We would be out there sounding (insulting) on each other's mothers, but David was never part of that. He was just a goofy big kid. He did all the stuff that we did and was always in the mix, but he never did anything controversial for us to get on him. He didn't bother anybody. He was quiet."

David's way of trying to communicate that he liked me was in how he looked at me and how he seized every opportunity to walk and talk with me when he caught me heading to one of the stores in our neighborhood. He did other little things too. Sometimes he would sit next to me on the benches, and I'm sure that we slow danced at some of the teen parties.

As Ronald said, David was always in the mix, but it's also true that he was never tethered to any particular clique in the projects. Sometimes he hung with my crew in "the middle," but he also associated with cliques in the back and the 102nd and 105th streets pods of East River Houses.

David was all over the place and may have had spoken or unspoken relationships with girls from other cliques, but I wouldn't know because he wasn't a kiss-and-tell kind of man. David kept many things about his relationships and his life in general to himself. Despite my curiosity, I learned not to pry too deeply and to respect who he was.

David's male acquaintances from back home that I was able to catch up with are fairly consistent in recollecting his personality as a young man.

The Frazier brothers, Michael and Sonny (aka A. Raheem Sami), for example, recalled David as being "cool," and Sonny very specifically described David as "reticent," meaning not one who readily reveals what he's thinking or feeling.

That fits with how I experienced David as a youth and as a man.

James Pendergrast, who was closer to David than many others, said that David characterized Aquarius, his astrological birth sign. "Dave was understanding and full of surprises as we grew into manhood," James said.

He recalled David being a counselor at Boy's Harbor, an East Harlem institution that Anthony Drexel Duke, a descendant of the fabulously wealthy Duke family, founded in 1937. Boys Harbor is co-ed today and offers many recreational and educational programs designed to help youth discover their talents.

David was also once a director of the community center in East Harlem's Robert Wagner projects, and while there, James, who was on the faculty at New York University, said that David hired him to work part time with the kids at the center.

"Dave was a humanitarian," James said. "He had an incredible heart, skills and a global outlook that was beautiful, but when we played chess — we were partners — you had to get a bucket to clean up the blood. We were two peas in a pod."

Again, James' recollection of David was in line with stories that Levet and other friends of David's shared about how he had given them good advice and how when he was in a position to do so, he hired them or inspired them.

Far from perfect, David would be the first to indict himself for mistakes that he made, but he was at heart a teacher and a friend, the kind of person one would want in a foxhole with them when bombs and bullets are flying. I wish I had known him better and stayed in touch over the years.

Back in the day, however, my dad would have made sure we didn't get too close. As I've said, my dad was no joke when it came to boys. "Get upstairs," he would yell if he saw anything, he just imagined was out of order involving me and a boy.

If I protested, "Daddy, you're embarrassing me," he would say, "Ask me if I care." When I saw that little muscle inside my father's cheeks begin to twitch, I knew that it was case closed and that whatever else I had to say was best left for another time.

Once I was old enough, my mother, the family psychologist and peacemaker, explained the likely root of Daddy's bad attitude toward boys sniffing around his three daughters. A couple of my father's sisters, Mommy said, had been in abusive relationships, and one of them, Aunt Margie, the only one of my father's sisters who I recall meeting, was shot and killed by her husband. Aunt Margie lived in New Jersey and was fed up with her husband. She decided to leave him once and for all and take her young son, Bobby, with her.

My aunt, my father and Uncle Gerald, the youngest brother, hatched an escape plan.

The way it was supposed to work is that Uncle Gerald would pick Aunt Margie and Bobby up at her house and drive them to Philadelphia to my godmother, who was also in on the plan. Aunt Margie would lay low in Philly for a few weeks and then make her way to her brothers in New York. The thinking was that our house would be the first place her husband would come looking.

Aunt Margie was packed and ready to run when her husband showed up unexpectedly brandishing a shotgun.

"Take one step, and I'll kill you," he reportedly said. She did, and he fired, killing my aunt in front of their son. Uncle Gerald pounced on him, but it was too late to save his sister. We don't know what prompted Aunt Margie's husband to come home early that day. He served time in prison for murder, but my father and Uncle Gerald, my mother said, were haunted by the fact that they weren't able save their sister. I cannot corroborate the finer details of what's become family lore because all who were directly involved, including my cousin Bobby, are deceased.

So, though I felt that my dad was unnecessarily wary when I was a young girl, and once I was grown, seemed to be unnecessarily critical of my choices in men, I understood that he was motivated by love.

As it happened, David and I would have had plenty of opportunities to flirt at the Church of the Ascension's chaperoned teen parties; after school at the East River Community Center; and when we were a little older, at the many 25 cents a head house parties in the projects. Some of the parties were given to raise money for my girls and me to buy sweaters bearing our names and the logo of our social club, "The Continental Queens." Our black, red and white sweaters matched those of our brothers, "The Continental Kings."

My mother and I had joined the United Presbyterian Church of the Ascension on 106th Street between First and Second avenues shortly after we moved to East Harlem in 1955. The church played an extraordinary role in our lives and those of many families living in East River projects. My father didn't go to church often, but every night he got down on his knees and prayed.

What made Ascension Church extra special was its affiliation with the East Harlem Protestant Parish. EHPP was founded in 1948 by Union Theological Seminary students who were passionate that Protestants should commit themselves to evangelizing and living in the midst of East Harlem's poor and dispossessed. EHPP was ecumenical and was supported by Methodists, Presbyterians, Congregationalists, Baptists, Evangelicals, the New York City Mission Society, the Union Theological Seminary, the Protestant Council and the National Council of Churches. Most EHPP ministries started in storefronts east of Lexington Avenue on 100, 102nd, 103rd and 104th streets and primarily serviced their African American and Puerto Rican neighbors.

Ascension began in a church building dating back to 1908 with an original mission to serve East Harlem's Italian immigrants. Many were still living in the neighborhood, but when EHPP took root, most of the Italians were affiliated with the Catholic churches that were abundant in East Harlem.

EHPP's progressive, grassroots approaches to urban ministry made it a magnet for many kind and brilliant seminarians, theologians and preachers. Lettie Russell, one of America's first ordained women, for example, pastored Ascension from 1959 to 1971. Katie Cannon, the first black woman ordained by the United Presbyterian Church in the United States of America, (before northern and southern Presbyterians merged), twice served Ascension's congregation. Charles Coleman, a Baptist, was affiliated with Ascension and lived in East River projects. Charles helped me to secure summer jobs in the United Presbyterian Church's Board of National Missions' file room when I was in high school. Years later, he became a dean at the historically black Shaw University in Raleigh, North Carolina. The school was founded by the American Baptist Home Mission Society in 1865, the same year that the Civil War ended.

Before George W. "Bill" Webber ascended to the presidency of New York Theological Seminary, he labored for years at Ascension Church and the EHPP. George raised his family in the Washington projects. His son, Thomas L. Webber, recalled those experiences in his 2004 book, "Flying over 96th Street: Memoir of an East Harlem White Boy."

George Todd, a Presbyterian whose World War II Army unit liberated a German concentration camp near Buchenwald, also served Ascension Church and raised his family in East Harlem. George would go on to help create and to lead ecumenical organizations in New York and Chicago. His social activism took him to World Council of Churches in Geneva, Switzerland, where his specialty was working with European churches to overcome the legacies of colonialism in India, Africa, Asia and Latin America.

The seminarians and the ministers who pastored and taught at Ascension and lived among congregants may have found their purpose in Jeremiah 29:7 (KJV) which says, "And seek the peace of the city whither I have caused you to be carried away captives, and pray unto the Lord for it: for in the peace thereof shall ye have peace."

Many of the young people that David and I grew up with, even ones who weren't Protestants, were immersed in a movement of Christian activism that helped to shape our world views and directly or indirectly impacted the careers many of us pursued as adults.

David is a case in point. He picked up invaluable skills as a community organizer and affordable housing specialist working for Hope Community, a project of the Church of the Good Hope, an EHPP member ministry. David earned certificates in the housing trades in courses offered at New York University. Though he had only a high school equivalency diploma at the time, David's deep knowledge of East Harlem led to him often supervising people with more academic credentials. Those skills that he amassed back home led him later in his life to employment managing small and large housing developments in Georgia, Florida and Puerto Rico.

As for me, growing up at Ascension, I was a sponge soaking up what was taught and modeled for me. The freedom school organized by the church's African American members in the early 1960s and the teen youth gatherings held at the Parish Acres retreat center, 60 miles outside the city, planted the seeds of social and political awareness. Helping to fill Christmas and Thanksgiving baskets with food and toys in the basement of Ascension imbued many of us with a commitment to public service and to have empathy and compassion for the neediest people in our community.

The seminarians who cycled through Ascension shared with us what they had seen, heard and experienced in their formal studies and mission trips abroad. Their talks, slide shows and field trips helped to offset the stereotypes in Tarzan, cowboys and Indians movies and yes, the racist cartoons, regularly featured on the big screen at the Eagle on Third Avenue. We may not have been required, as was true for our Southern relatives, to sit in segregated "crow's nests" at the movies, but we were nevertheless being programmed by Hollywood to root against the people on the screen who looked like us.

My mother sang in the choir at Ascension. I have memories of that little choir two-stepping down the center aisle singing more like Baptists than Presbyterians. Mom also occasionally hosted Bible studies in our apartment. My father came home in the middle of one Bible study, looked around the room, and asked my mom to excuse herself for a minute. "Tell those white people to take their feet off my furniture," Daddy said. They meant no harm, I'm sure, and Mommy didn't do what Daddy instructed, but he was really offended.

When I was old enough, I served on Ascension's governing body, and in the early 1970s, I directed the church's youth ministry. I invited friends to teach the kids dance and sandal making. I raised money for field trips like going to see the film "Sounder" about a family of sharecroppers in Louisiana. My hope was that they would learn something from the movie and that the knowledge that Cicely Tyson, the movie's co-star, had also once lived in East Harlem would inspire them.

When I moved to Louisville, I joined St. Stephen Baptist Church in 1991 precisely because it opened its doors to the community seven days a week and had programming for children, seniors, ex-addicts, ex-cons, individuals and families in distress that reminded me of the Presbyterian Church of the Ascension.

Sometime in the mid-1970s faced with a declining membership and budget, Ascension lost its building. Connie Williams Gant, who also grew up in Ascension and is still active, recalled the congregation moving to a storefront on Third Avenue and 106th Street. Katie Cannon pastored the storefront congregation for four or five years, Connie said. After Katie moved on, Fred Davies, the new pastor, encouraged a merger between Ascension and the also struggling Mt. Morris Presbyterian Church on 122nd Street, and so was born the Mt. Morris Ascension Presbyterian Church.

For sticklers, I should note that the EHPP tradition was not to call our pastors and leaders by their titles. We knew they had degrees, but everyone was on a first-name basis. I assume that the intent, when EHPP was formed, was that there would be no artificial barriers between the leaders and the people they were called to lead. The former Ascension building is now the home of the Macedonia Iglesia Pentecostal Church, a Spanish-language congregation. That congregation generously allows former Ascension families to hold funerals for their loved ones in the church. Katie Cannon preached my father's funeral at Macedonia Iglesia in 1983.

If the walls of that old church house could talk, they would have quite a story to tell about all the different ethnic groups that settled in East Harlem and left their mark.

When I met David at the reunion, he was living in Pittsburgh. He had driven to New York City to visit family and in particular, he told me later, to see his stepson Sonny's newborn twin girls.

Unfortunately, I didn't have David's undivided attention for long. Old friends who also hadn't seen him in years gathered 'round to greet him. "Dave, you look good, man," said one. Another asked, "Where you been? Ain't seen you in like forever."

David basked in the warm greetings, and I fell back waiting to get his attention again. When his old amigos drifted away, David and I found a spot a little way off from the reunion crowd to sit and talk. That's when I really got a good look at the grown-up David. My Puerto Rican heartthrob was still, as we used to say, fine as wine and mellow as a cello.

The stocky, young David Rivera was now barrel-chested and thick around the waist, but it worked on his frame. His bright white T-shirt complimented his skin, which was smooth and tanned the color of coffee with a nice dollop of sweet cream. His black baseball cap could not mask that his once large Afro halo had gone the way of the buffalo.

We caught up on our lives for a couple of hours until David excused himself. He promised to circle back after making his own rounds in the neighborhood seeing old friends. As good as his word, David did make it back to the Big Park. By then, the reunion was winding down. The cleanup was under way, and the big crowd had scattered leaving people to socialize in small clusters throughout the projects.

David and I left the park together and stood talking outside my sister Debbie's building on 102nd Street. By then, we had estimated that we hadn't seen one another in nearly 50 years. He remained in

East Harlem for many years after I had moved to the Bronx. He was still living there in the mid-70s when I moved back and into Lakeview, a new development on 107th Street and Fifth Avenue, across from Central Park. My rent-subsidized, two-bedroom, 22nd floor apartment had a balcony and an unobstructed, high-rent view across one of the park's lakes and the old boathouse at 110th Street. Frederick Law Olmsted (1822-1903), hailed as "the father of American landscape, was the visionary behind New York's Central Park as well as many other grand urban oases in the United States. At night, the street lights, the apartment lights and the lights on the East River bridges twinkled like diamonds set in a giant necklace across East Harlem, Harlem and the Upper West Side. My views were breathtaking.

I could walk from Lakeview to my parents' apartment in the projects. In 1983, on Father's Day, I walked those eight blocks to deliver the news to my mother that her husband, my Daddy, was dead. The hospital called me, because I was the contact person on file. I remember sliding down to the floor still holding the phone and struggling to comprehend the meaning of "expired." I could have driven to the projects, but I walked in the blazing heat, sobbing and being angry that people I passed in the streets were going about their business as though nothing had happened.

Didn't they know? Didn't they care that the most important man in my life was dead? I wanted the world to stop just for a few minutes to mourn with me and to pay tribute. My father was only 59 years old, younger than I am now. He was a victim of the cigarettes that he had learned to smoke when he was kid back in Virginia.

When I got to my mother's and told her, she did not seem surprised. She said that she knew that the end was near the day before Daddy died.

My nephew, Larry, Debbie's son, was standing outside the ground floor window of my father's room. He was too young to visit his grandfather. I told Daddy that Larry was outside and directed his face toward the window. The sun was so bright that I doubt that he could actually see Larry. Daddy could no longer talk, but he moved his lips and said, "Hit a home run for me." My nephews, Larry and Darnell, Georgeann's son, spent hours hanging out with my dad. Daddy called both boys Woody, after Woody Woodpecker, the cartoon character. He would sneak them dollars and quarters and instruct them not to tell their mothers. They had lots of secrets, we learned much later. When his failing health forced him to retire, Daddy would walk the boys to school. He relished saying, "My grandsons."

A few days after Daddy died, Debbie and I went back to thank the staff at Bird S. Coler Hospital on Roosevelt Island, a narrow strip in the East River. Daddy was transferred to Coler after his oncologist at Metropolitan Hospital, the one closest to our house, could no longer justify keeping him there, where he had been placed to accommodate our family's daily presence.

"Are you Mr. Winston's daughters?" a nurse asked. "Yes," we replied. She said that she was my father's nurse, and she told Debbie and I an amazing story of his passing.

"I don't know how he did it," she said, "but your father managed to get out of bed and into a wheelchair. He or someone wheeled him into the bathroom where he washed his face. He rolled back to his room but didn't have the strength to get back into bed. I picked him up and was holding him, and he died in my arms. He died like a saint."

Debbie and I wept at the telling, but part of me believed that the nurse simply wanted to comfort us. We went and told Mommy what the nurse had said, and she didn't believe it either. Daddy was so weakened by cancer that we couldn't imagine him being able to get out of bed on his own. We could believe, however, that Daddy wanted to wash himself up. He was always meticulous about his appearance. Anyhow, when we unpacked the big plastic bag that contained Daddy's belongings, there was among the items, a crumpled-up face cloth that was still a little damp.

After David and I got together, he shared with me that he actually hung out with my dad and his friends on "the squares," a spot on 106th Street between First Avenue and the East River Drive, where men gathered to shoot the breeze, argue about World War II, and drink their pleasure out of brown paper bags.

I should have run into David during the years that I lived in Lakeview. I had passed the places that he lived and hung out hundreds of times, but never met up with him.

East Harlem's population is larger than that of many cities, but it was also a village stabilized by branches of families like David's and mine that remained in the old 'hood long after most of the children had graduated, married and moved away.

David said he moved around in New York for a few years before seeking new adventures Puerto Rico, Florida and Georgia. He lived in Georgia two or three different times and said he hoped one day to move back to the Atlanta metro area. He moved to Pittsburgh, the hometown of his longtime girlfriend, Diane, from whom he said he was now estranged. I learned that David previously had a wild, short-lived marriage, two grown children, a daughter and a son, and a granddaughter from each of his kids. Mostly, he managed apartment complexes in the cities where he lived and decided to go into partnership with Diane flipping houses in Pittsburgh. Like the personal relationship, the business relationship didn't work out. By the time we met up at the reunion, David was working overnight in a group home for mentally challenged men.

David eventually got around to asking if I was married or otherwise romantically involved. When I said no, he swore that the last time he saw me I was wearing a wedding gown. He said he happened to be passing by the place where my reception was being held and saw me. He said he walked over and whispered, "One day, you'll come back to me."

I have no such recollection of that, but if David did see me that day, it was in October 1966, when I married Brian Collier McCrary. I was working as a secretary, the career I prepared for at Benjamin Franklin High School. I graduated from Franklin in 1963 with awards for stenography and typing.

Brian and I were married at my family church, the United Presbyterian Church of the Ascension, on 106th Street. Our wedding reception was back in the projects in the day-care center where my mother worked. The center has a fenced-in outdoor area, visible to passers-by, so it is very possible that David saw and spoke to me that day.

If I'm not mistaken, I met Brian the summer between my junior and senior year at Franklin. A year older than I, he lived on 99th Street "over the coast," meaning on the other side of the elevated Metro North Railroad tracks on Park Avenue. I don't recall where he went to school. My senior yearbook recorded Betty Winston's "favorite thing" as "blue-eyed boys." I was not referring to white boys, and I went to school with plenty of them, but to Brian. He was a very fair-skinned African American with blue eyes. Both his parents were black, but clearly someone on his family tree was white; how many generations back, man or woman, I cannot say.

What I can say is that by the time I graduated, yearbook notwithstanding, Brian was no longer my "favorite thing." We had drifted apart during my senior year. He reappeared in late 1965 when someone told him that I was in the hospital. Pneumonia nearly killed me, and Brian rode in like a handsome prince on his gallant steed. He came to rescue me, and I was smitten. Based on pure emotion, and little else, I decided that I was in love, and so when Brian proposed while I was in the hospital, I quickly said, "Yes."

Several of my girlfriends from the neighborhood and high school were getting married around the same time, so I figured that I would get married too and borrowed a wedding gown from Barbara Shirley, my Ben Franklin High School classmate, who had gotten married a year or two earlier.

I invested more time in planning the wedding than thinking about whether either of us was ready to be married. Many people married at our ages, 19 and 20, including my parents, and have had long successful marriages, but in our case, Brian and I were not ready. My father did not want me to marry Brian. Daddy learned to like Brian, though the color thing — his near whiteness and my very darkness — worried him. He feared that if we ever got into arguments, Brian would call me ugly names with reference to my color. "Colorism" is a persistent issue among African-descended people. It's a wretched holdover from colonialism in Africa and slavery and Jim Crow in America. Light-skinned black people, who were the offspring of the colonizers and slaveholders seemed to get preferred treatment. The "Black Power Movement" mitigated some of the sting of colorism, but the vestiges of the divisions remained and unfortunately were often perpetrated by such customs as "the paper bag test." If you were darker than a brown paper bag, you were liable to be excluded from certain African American social organizations. If you were my complexion, certain parents, both light and dark-skinned, were suspicious of your motives if you decided to marry into the family. Brian wasn't into that, and he never hit me with color-based slurs. As for me, I just thought that he was cute and funny and most important, he really loved me.

So, while my Dad grew comfortable with Brian being around, he thought I could do better for a husband. I was dressed for the wedding and was primping in the mirror when my father slipped up behind me and asked, "Are you pregnant?" I said, "Oh, Daddy. I'm not pregnant." I'll never forget his response, "So, you're just marrying him for no reason!" That actually wasn't far from the truth. Brian and I had no good reason to get married. Other than our feelings, we didn't have much in common. I had been a good student, and I was ambitious. Brian, on the other hand, was an around-the-way kind of guy. He wasn't into education, long-term planning and such. He lived in the moment, and I guess figured that life would just take care of itself. He wasn't on any career track. Brian was a hustler. He took whatever work he could get, and to be sure, the jobs he did manage to find in construction or in the Garment Center downtown didn't pay much.

I hated to disappoint my father, and I ended up being late for my own wedding listening to him try his best to talk me out of it. He even said he would go to the church to announce that the wedding was off, but I couldn't stop the show. My friends and family, some of who had come from out of town, were there waiting at the church. Not only that, but the food had been purchased and prepared, and Mical Whitaker, a teacher at the day-care center, who later founded the East Harlem Players Theater Company, had decorated the reception area with fall flowers and leaves. Back at the church, Brian and his best man, Earl Phinze, were waiting too.

Daddy eventually stopped trying to talk me out of what I was about to do. With a grimace on his face, he walked me down the aisle. When the preacher, the Rev. Lettie Russell, asked, "Who giveth this bride away?" my father didn't answer at first, and then I'm sure I heard him whisper, "Um!" I'm not sure if Lettie heard him, but she proceeded as if he had said, "I do."

I wasn't the happiest bride-to-be, but I had to go through with the wedding. Part of me was miserable because of my father's disapproval on what should have been a happy day. Daddy was right to oppose the marriage. It was short-lived because, though Brian and I cared deeply for one another, we were too immature to be husband and wife. We were "playing house." Sometimes Brian would turn the lights out in our apartment and then pop out of the darkness. He would widen his blue eyes and pounce on me laughing manically as if he was Bela Lugosi, the Hungarian-American actor who terrified legions of movie-goers as Count Dracula.

The most ridiculous stunt Brian pulled was the day I apparently wasn't giving him enough attention, so he "shot" himself. He dropped to the floor and to make his "suicide" seem more authentic he dribbled hot sauce on his shirt. My 11-year-old sister, Georgeann, who was visiting us, was hysterical. "Brian's dead! Brian's dead!" I struggled to assure her that he was faking. I kept stepping over him, "When he gets tired of lying there he'll get up," I said. My sister was relieved when Brian ended his little charade, but she was upset with her brother-in-law for scaring her like that. I'm sure I did some silly things too, but I don't remember being quite as silly as my husband.

Our marriage ended amicably in less than a year. I concluded that we had no future and decided to move out. We remained friends for the rest of Brian's life and he stayed close to my family. My sisters adored him. He died suddenly in the early 1980s. I was remarried by then. I was told that Brian's heart just stopped beating. As far as I know, he never married again, but he did have two children, a son and a daughter, with a longtime girlfriend.

Meanwhile, back at the Old Timers' Reunion, when I told David that I didn't have a special man at that time, a light snapped on in his handsome face, and he stepped up his rap and moved in for the kill. It was charming. It had been a while since a man had given me that sort of attention.

Nevertheless, the hour was late, and I was truly one exhausted old broad. My legs ached, and my mind was yelling at me to get some rest. I also had to catch a train back to D.C. the next morning. David and I parted with friendly hugs and smooches. We promised to keep in touch. Riding the elevator up to my sister's apartment, I was genuinely happy to have seen my boy crush again. He looked great.

The next morning, I slid into my seat on the train and reflected on the day before. I wondered, perhaps, maybe, wouldn't it be nice, if love could have found me once more. I understood, of course, that my reconnection with David easily could end up being one sweet day-trip down memory lane. Would he really stay in touch? I hoped so. I also hoped that he would call while I was on the train. He didn't, and I tried to soothe my wounded ego, telling myself that this wouldn't be the first time that I had totally misread a man's signals. Doubts engulfed me like a heavy funeral shroud. I told myself that even if David never called, it really was great seeing him again, given that many of our mutual childhood friends had not survived East Harlem's mean streets. They were dead, in jail or in terrible health after years of substance abuse or just from being too poor to afford healthcare or good nutrition.

If we were nothing else, David and I were survivors.

By the time my train pulled into Union Station in D.C., I had fortified myself for the letdown. I was after all a grown woman.

The next day, David called to say, "I was with my family and got caught up. But I was thinking about you."

"You were?" I cooed.

Even if that wasn't true, it was a sweet thing for David to say. He was reeling me in. After that, we talked everyday several times a day. Sometimes our late-night calls lasted so long that I would doze off, and he would call me on my other phone and say, "Hang up. I'll call you tomorrow." We were two 60-some-year-olds acting like teenagers burning up the phone lines.

After weeks of daily phone calls, David and I were ready to explore whether what we thought we were feeling for one another was real, and if so, what were we prepared to do about it. Neither of us wanted to move too quickly or so slowly that we might miss our moment. We needed more time together to test the waters.

Chapter 3

Apaga la Luz - (La India)

No, he didn't, I thought when David unpacked his car and pulled a boom box and a bunch of CDs out of the trunk along with our suitcases. I imagined some snarky millennials passing through the hotel parking lot and laughing. "Look at Grandma and Grandpa about to get their thing on. What y'all you got in that stack? The *original* Temptations?" I imagined a snappy comeback to the youngins': "As a matter of fact, we are about to get our thing on, and guess what, young 'don't last always. Keep living."

David may have been toting old technology, but it was thoughtful of him to bring *our* kind of music, grown folks' music, to help set the mood for our weekend rendezvous, our first face-to-face since we renewed old acquaintances at East River projects Old Timers' Reunion, in New York a month earlier. I was eager to see him again, and so, I had invited him to the annual fall crab fest hosted by the Veterans of Foreign Wars in Westminster, Maryland. My mom, Betty Jane Brown, graduated from Westminster's segregated Robert Moten High School in 1944. My cousin Ronald Hollingsworth, a Vietnam Vet who served two tours, usually reserves a table for our family and friends. The grands, great-grands and great-great-grands of Ed and Roxie Brown, my maternal grandparents, loved to work our way through piles of hard-shell crabs and Maryland sweet white corn.

David drove from Pittsburgh and picked me up at Baltimore-Washington International Airport. He rolled up to the curb in his white, '97 Toyota Avalon. David loved his car with the odometer that stopped working at 275,000 miles. Other than a dead battery, the Toyota was still operable when he died in 2015. After more than a year of letting it sit for sentimental reasons, I donated the car to a struggling young mother with two small children. David would have been pleased. I asked the young lady if she would like to see a photo of the man who had owned the car. She didn't. I guess she thought she would be spooked by David's spirit. I handed over the keys and didn't press the matter.

Despite our many late-night calls that often ended with one or both of us saying, "Can't wait to see you again," when David and I were finally face-to-face in Maryland, we were self-conscious and not quite sure what to expect. There were so many what ifs.

It was about a 25-minute drive from our hotel to Westminster where the crab fest was to be held the next day. David said that he had not inherited his mother's fondness for the hard-shelled crustaceans for which Maryland is famous, but he wanted to be with me.

After we dropped our bags in our room, David pulled me close. He was a big man. He wrapped 4-foot, 11-inch me in his arms, leaned down and kissed me. Then, famished after our travels, David and I left our hotel in search of food. We found a nearly abandoned mall nearby. The large anchor stores were closed, but a few holdouts occupied what seemed to have once been a vibrant food court.

Our choices were limited, and we settled on Mexican fare. The choice turned out to be my introduction to what I call David's *mi hermano* (my brother) shtick. Whenever he encountered other Spanish speakers, no matter their country of origin, David instantly connected with them. The guys working the counter weren't Puerto Ricans, or even Mexicans. They were from somewhere in Central America and were visibly thrilled and smiled lavishly when David began talking to them in Spanish.

David was their *hermano* of a slightly darker hue. Thanks to colonization and the Atlantic slave trade, the folks often referred to as Hispanics or Latinos come in all colors; from the whitest of white with the straightest of straight hair, to the blackest of black with the nappiest of nappy hair. Sometimes, all those colors and hair textures exist in the same biological family.

Of course, I had no idea what David and his newfound brothers were yakking about. "They're Guatemalans," he said when he arrived back at the table toting over-stuffed take-out boxes, enough to feed six, I calculated.

That was one of many occasions when David and I clearly got much more than we paid for or expected simply because he connected with other Latinos. He was always friendly to the so-called menial laborers: the janitors, hotel maids, fast-food jockeys and the lawn keepers.

One day, I overheard David counseling a Mexican landscaper about the man's immigration papers. The slim, brown-skinned man apparently trusted David enough to talk to him about his status. What did David know about immigration, I wondered, since Puerto Ricans are U.S. citizens? Puerto Rico is an American territory. Americans don't need passports or visas to travel there and vice-versa. The reality is that it was David's nature to try to help people. I suspect that he and the man had talked previously and that David had either talked to somebody or had done his own research on his computer. David's instinct to help appealed to me. Anyhow, when I came home a few days later, flowers had been planted in the previously weed-choked little patch behind the condo, apparently a sign of the landscaper's gratitude.

In Maryland, once we were back to the hotel, we ate, and David made a quick trip back downstairs, probably to smoke a joint, but I didn't mention it when he came back to the room. He slid CDs into their slots in his boombox, our private party was on.

We two-stepped, did a few Latin dances and a little cheek-to-cheek. We reminisced about how Manhattan and the Bronx were popping when we were young adults with ballrooms, nightclubs, piano bars, holes-in-the wall, and one-way-in, one-way-out joints that catered to connoisseurs of jazz, soul and Latin music. David and I had traveled in different circles and never ran into each other, but we remembered doing a lot of the same things. In those days, for a few bucks, we were able see the greats of all those genres up close. We recalled how we would party with different friends into the wee hours, working up sweats and appetites that we satiated at cafes and restaurants that catered to night owls. My favorite late-night spot was Wells' on Seventh Avenue. Wells' was the blueprint for other chicken and waffle houses that have sprung up from Los Angeles to Atlanta and all points in between.

Wells' Supper Club opened in Harlem in 1938. At Wells', mere mortals might find ourselves on any given weekend eating one table over from famous entertainers, poets and writers. Nat King Cole and Maria Cole held a wedding reception at Wells'. Though I never ran into them, I'm told that James Baldwin and Sammy Davis Jr. were frequent patrons. Speaking of Davis, one of my great aspirations after high school was to meet somebody who knew somebody who would tell Sammy Davis to hire me as his personal assistant. It never happened. I always liked Davis as a performer and admired his glamorous lifestyle.

To be honest, Harlem wasn't shining nearly as brightly as it did when my parents met there in the early 1940s. Absentee landlords and drugs were taking a toll, but when I finally was old enough to hang out and go clubbing in the mid-60s, I saw vestiges of the days when the good times rolled, and Harlem was home to happy feet.

David and I talked about the kings and queens of salsa; for example, Celia Cruz, Tito Puente, Johnny Pacheco, Mongo Santamaria, Willie Bobo, Joe Bataan and Johnny Colon. They were as down to earth as their music was sweet and funky. The bawdy and naughty Cuban singer La Lupe, with her boss singing and antics, was quite a character. I was such a wild woman on the dance floor at the Palladium nightclub that some of my friends started calling me La Lupe. In my heyday, I really could dance. After all, I grew up in El Barrio, East Harlem's other name, and I loved Latin music, culture and boys. When it comes to that music, one need not understand Spanish to be swept away by the feeling. Ladies, you have not danced until some fine *papi chulo* (a cutie) has bent your back to the sexy Puerto-Rican inspired sounds of singers like Jimmy Sabater and Cheo Feliciano.

That weekend in Maryland, and every day we shared thereafter, David Rivera played the music that made me dance. He wasn't every woman's kind of man, and likely wouldn't have been the man for me at other stages of my life, but in the season that he showed up, he was right on time as a lover and a friend. He was with me when I felt vulnerable and misunderstood. He made me laugh when I wanted to cry. He was home.

If anyone had reason to peek into the window of our hotel room that weekend in Maryland, they wouldn't have seen two 60-something-year-olds, but two young adults having a ball. We were like the Charles Whitley character in Rod Serling's "Twilight Zone" episode, "Kick the Can" in 1962 that takes place in the Sunnyvale Rest Home.

Whitley, a retiree, believed that the secret of youth was to act young, so he invited other residents of the old folks' home to play the children's game Kick the Can. Once they began to play, Whitley and his companions were young again. They had no aches, pains or complaints. They were free.

When La India's "Apaga la Luz," a Latin remake of Teddy Pendergrass' "Turn Off the Lights," came through the speakers of David's boombox, my first evening alone with David went to a higher level. I loved the song when Teddy sang it but hadn't heard La India's remake and had David play it several times.

We were having a great time, but the hour had gotten really late and my knees needed a break from dancing. I pulled out of my suitcase the pretty robe with the matching teddy and panties that I had bought for the occasion.

My intent was to impress. I danced into the bathroom. The shower was hot and almost medicinal after a very long day. I hung out under the water much longer than necessary to get clean. The shower rejuvenated me. I got out, splashed a couple drops of cologne on my neck and behind my ears. The silky robe felt good next to my skin, and then with my best Eartha Kitt impersonation, I emerged from the bathroom purring and trailed by the billowing steam unleashed by my long, hot shower. Like a scene from the classic film, "Sunset Boulevard," in which a former Hollywood actress desperately dreams of a comeback, I was ready for my close-up.

To my horror, David looked at me and laughed. It wasn't the response I had anticipated. My ego deflated like a balloon pricked by a pin. OK, so I wasn't the skinny Betty of my youth, but a joke? I was livid, and by the way, who the hell was David with the bald head and jelly belly to laugh at me. I wanted him to take off his clothes so I could have a good laugh, too.

It quickly dawned on David that I didn't get the joke, so he steered me back into the bathroom and stood me before the mirror. The steam had evaporated by then, and Lord have mercy, no wonder he laughed. I looked a hot mess. My face was streaked with mascara from the shower. I looked like a raccoon bandit. At that point, I had to laugh too, and the crisis passed.

David took his turn in the bathroom and afterward it was *apaga la luz,* or in English, lights out. After weeks of late-night telephone romancing and promises that fireworks would go off once we got hold of one another, the time had come to put up or shut up. We lay side by side in the king-sized bed. David pulled me close in the middle, and we kissed and kissed some more. Even in the pitch darkness, I sensed his anxiousness, indeed his eagerness, to live up to his boasts. Needless to say, David and I didn't come of age in the social media and reality television era where hardly anything is left to imagination, so I'm blushing as I write this and suspect that David would actually not be blushing, but quite possibly annoyed.

However, to be as transparent as a woman my age can be, and some might argue, should be, I'll say that that night in Maryland was the first time that David and I were together in that way. We may have arrived with general ideas of what we wanted or what we hoped to get from one another. but neither he nor I knew what to expect. Nevertheless, we pushed past our initial shyness, uncertainty and awkwardness until we found a rhythm that worked for us. Our shyness wasn't just that it was about to be our first time, but David and I had packed on pounds over five decades, so we didn't exactly have beach bodies. We were more we akin to beach balls.

I also have arthritis in my lower back, so it goes without saying that the bedroom acrobatics of more youthful lovers were out of the question. Our first time wasn't anything akin to the book and the movie "Fifty Shades of Grey," but we were happy. Afterward, David was pleased with himself, and it wasn't long before he was snoring like a train going south. I lay there in the darkness thinking about how old friends had become new lovers, and I swear that I heard Etta James off in the distance singing, "At Last."

After my weekend in Maryland with David, I flew back to Louisville assured that I should take a chance on falling again for an old friend with whom I had history and much in common. David was steadily snaking his way into my head and my heart. Whenever I pass a Hyatt Place Hotel, I recall that sweet September weekend in Maryland when David and I came full circle. I had felt safe in David's bear hug. I have a particular fondness for men who make me feel safe. I've had men who've cared for me, and men who may have even loved me, but their responses and actions, unwittingly signaled to me that my life with them, in critical moments, would still leave me vulnerable and on my own.

I trace my need to feel safe in intimate relationships directly to my father. My father always made me feel safe. I literally did not realize, until he was in the casket, that my Dad really wasn't seven feet tall. He wasn't even 6 feet tall. Safety, in my case, isn't purely a matter of a man's height, width or size. It's a matter of his heart. On that score, my father was as tall as a sequoia. He was an imperfect man. He drank too much sometimes and occasionally he broke my mother's heart, but my father never gave me or my sisters any reason to doubt that his love for us, and his desire to protect us was steadfast and unequivocal. Every girl should experience that. Until the day that my father died, I was his "Boopie Girl" and his "Papoose." My mother embedded in my head and heart a very important message: "Your daddy loves you."

When I was grown and tried to question my mother about how she endured my father's faults and the rumors about my father and other women, I'll never forget what she said to me, "He's your father, but he's my man." In other words, that part of their relationship was none of my business and should have no bearing whatsoever on how I felt about my father or he about me.

I had seen my mother fighting tears on many Fridays waiting for Daddy to come home with his pay, but she never ran my father down. My mother was an extraordinary woman and a wise counselor. Though our family struggled, my mother never ran back to her parents in Maryland. She toughed it out and was often heard to say, "I made my bed hard, and so I have to lay in it."

Chapter 4

You Ought to Be with Me - (Al Green)

That Maryland weekend wasn't enough. David and I desperately craved more face time. Those daily long-distance phone calls weren't getting it, and so a few weeks later, my man was on an airplane heading to Louisville.

David apparently was talking me up to a woman he met in the airport, and I was surprised that she called me a few days later. She said that David had given her my phone number. "Really," I thought. "Oh, yes," she said, "He talked about you the whole trip and about how you grew up together and got back together after all those years."

The woman was almost breathless. "It was sweet to hear a man talking about his woman in such glowing terms. He must really love you. It was really sweet." I thanked her with a neck and an eye roll that, of course, she couldn't see.

Miss Thing seemed a little too eager and much too interested in our business, and I told David as much. "I think girlfriend was hitting on you." If I met a stranger on a plane, even if he gave me his woman's number, it would never occur to me to call her.

"No. No. She was just being nice," David insisted.

I didn't press the matter, but I couldn't believe that an old player like David was oblivious to a sister making a move on him. I can smell a cougar from a mile away. It's a woman thing that I'm sure most women of a certain age can understand. The black man pool is pretty shallow when one is young, but it's nearly empty for black women 50 and over. Surely, I'm not the only woman who notices how quickly older men get snatched up after their wives have died and that often the circling piranha, the fresh-water fish famous for its sharp teeth and powerful jaws, are friends of his dearly departed life partner. Though I didn't appreciate that stranger calling to vouch for David, it wasn't worth arguing about. We laughed about it later.

David stayed a week, and I showed him around Louisville. I drove him through some of the city's neighborhoods. I took him through Old Louisville, which gets it lifeblood from the University of

Louisville students who occupy campus housing and many of the brownstones nearby. We rode around the Highlands with its tree-lined streets, trendy restaurants and stately old mansions. I gave him a quick tour of Butchertown, the funky district, notable for classic "shotgun" style homes and former meatpacking houses that have found new life as apartments, pubs and small businesses.

I drove him past my former home, the first that I ever owned, in West Louisville's historic Russell neighborhood, and I gave him a tour of my church, St. Stephen Baptist, located in the California neighborhood of West Louisville. He thoroughly enjoyed visiting the Muhammad Ali Center, which overlooks the mighty Ohio River and Southern Indiana. Finally, I took David to one of my favorite spots in the city, the Abraham Lincoln Memorial in Waterfront Park. He was impressed by the memorial, which features a 12-foot statue of young Lincoln, book in hand, seated on a rock, with his signature top hat perched beside him, looking out at the Ohio. Ed Hamilton, who sculpted the magnificent tribute to the 16th President of the United States, is a longtime friend.

Ed is a beautiful soul. The backstory of this particular Lincoln commission was inspired, he said at the dedication, by young Lincoln's visit to Louisville in 1841. Lincoln and Joshua Speed were down by the Ohio when the future president was reportedly captivated by the spectacle of a dozen enslaved people about to be transported down river to New Orleans. Years later, Lincoln wrote to Speed and said, "That sight was a continual torment to me; and I see something like it every time I touch the Ohio, or any other slave-border."

Experiencing David in my adopted city and in my space during his visit endeared him to me all the more. I was growing increasingly comfortable with the notion that he might be a keeper. He made me laugh, and he had elephantine memories of East Harlem. He was my homie.

I had lived in Louisville since 1984 and made a good life and great friends, but none of them knew much about my life before I moved there. They knew me as a journalist and a club member, but I didn't go to elementary, high school or college with them. I'm active in the Louisville Chapter of Delta Sigma Theta Sorority Inc., but none of my sorors here were initiated with me into Epsilon Tau, the New York city-wide chapter, in the spring of 1978.

I moved to Louisville to be a reporter for *The Courier-Journal*, and I re-created myself, not because I didn't love myself, but because that's what one does when one dares to move hundreds of miles from home. I confess that I sometimes get lonely for my family: my two sisters, my nieces, my nephews and my cousins back on the East Coast. I'm lonely for people who knew me when, who knew my mother and father, and who are familiar with the environment that helped to shape my attitudes and personality. Sometimes, I desperately miss the multi-cultural vibe of New York.

Obviously, I had a lot to learn about David and he about me because we hadn't seen or spoken with one another in years. Simply put, we had a lot of catching up and filling in to do.

We had both been married, me twice, and had failed at it. As I got to know him better, I realized that it wasn't in David's nature to make a lot of excuses for the things he had done and the choices he made during the decades we were out of touch. I never heard anything good or bad about David during those years, so I was in no position to judge him.

He definitely had regrets, a few of which he shared with me. David owned up to being an addict earlier in his life, but as he said with a certain amount of pride, "I was never a bum. I never robbed people's mother's pocketbooks."

David told me that he kicked his heroin habit on his own, cold turkey, because methadone, the synthetic drug he was prescribed, presumably to ease his withdrawal, made him sick. "I just traded one addiction for another. I hated it."

I wasn't shocked by David's substance abuse. More than a few of our mutual East Harlem childhood friends, boys and girls, went down that path. Many died young from overdoses, AIDS or the violence that accompanies that lifestyle.

For example, one weekday afternoon I spied one of my close childhood friends prostituting under the Metro North Railroad tracks near 125th Street. She had gotten hooked after high school. I pretended not to see her because I knew that she wouldn't have wanted me to see her on her job. I got word a few years later that she had died and left two young children behind. David recalled the occasion when one of his best friend's younger sister, a beautiful girl, offered to give him a "blow job" for a few dollars. "She was so high she didn't even recognize me," he said.

He acknowledged that he had intentionally or not, hurt people who loved him. He hurt his mother who adored him and lived with the constant fear, he said, that her "Davy" would end up dead in the streets or in prison. He hurt his children, Liza and David Levet, and their mothers, Saundra and Juanita. He wasn't there for them emotionally when they needed him to be a presence. Liza may have suffered the most. Though they were in touch, they were in some ways estranged. "I can't get through to her," David said sadly after one of their phone conversations. He could be a better man, but he couldn't undo the past.

David's relationship with his children was complicated, but at least David had children: a daughter, a son and two granddaughters. Whether he was the best father, a great father, a good father or a schmuck, is for others to judge. Through his children and grandchildren, David has a legacy. He has at least two people who look like him and who inherited, not just his genes, but elements of his personality.

I, on the other hand, am childless. When I die, it really will be over. My nieces and nephews love me, but I will leave no mini-me and no one who can truthfully say that I was the best mother ever or one that never should have had a child.

Not having a child isn't something that I talk about very much. I've certainly thought about it. After David died, his son said to me, "Look what you've gotten out of the deal. A son!" It made me feel so good.

Many years ago, I briefly contemplated adoption and sought the wise counsel of my mother, my best friend. Mom and I discussed the pros and cons of adoption. Two things about that conversation so many years ago stand out to me. First, my mother instructed me never to be jealous because my younger sisters have children and I don't. She always seemed to know the right thing to say in the right moments.

"You will have many children," my mother said, seeming to anticipate, though I was still in my 20s, what has actually occurred. I do have many children. They are young people that I've mentored or informally adopted and welcomed into my life as my extended family. My mother assured me, and I had no reason to believe otherwise, that childless women have important roles to play in advancing families and societies.

Mostly though, Mom talked to me that day and many times after, about the sacrifices she believed a woman who gets pregnant, by choice or accident, is required to make once she gives birth. Based on my lifestyle at the time, Mom wasn't sure these were sacrifices I would be willing to make. "A child isn't like a bag of laundry. You can't drop the baby off and run," she said. Moreover, Mom made it perfectly clear that she wasn't about to become a permanent babysitter.

It occurs to me that perhaps, a tiny perhaps, my mom was talking to me but thinking about the choices and sacrifices she had made. Maybe she was thinking how different, and maybe even better, her life might have been had she gone to Maryland State Teachers College at Bowie. She had been a good student and had been accepted to the college, but instead of going to Bowie, Mom headed north to New York. She caught the first thing smoking out of Union Bridge, Maryland shortly after graduating high school in 1944. World War II was raging, and my mother's brother, my Uncle Joe, was in the thick of it. He was in the Army fighting on the front lines in Italy and North Africa. Mom, the youngest of Ed and Roxie Brown's 10 children, eight of whom survived into adulthood, would have been the first in her family to go to college. Mom becoming a teacher would have been a very big deal indeed. In those years, black teachers were cherished and respected. Uncle Joe wanted that so much that he sent instructions from the war zones that some portion of his military allotment was to be set aside for Mom's education. But it wasn't to be.

Mom went to visit my Aunt Catherine, who was living on Harlem's fabled Sugar Hill. She wasn't in the big city very long before she met my father at a nightclub on Eighth Avenue. Harlem was on and popping, Mom always said. She was starry-eyed and would never live in Maryland again. Union Bridge could hardly compete with the bright lights and the excitement of *Sugar Hill*.

Uncle Joe, meanwhile, was beside himself when he learned that Mom didn't return to Maryland to go to school. He stopped speaking to her for a time, Mom said. If Uncle Joe was put out, my grandfather was worse. He was angry and mortified that his college-bound baby girl had taken up, as he saw it, with some fast-talking "city slicker."

Actually, my dad had migrated to Harlem from Richmond, Virginia, in the 1940s. He fled Richmond, he always said, because he despised its racism and all those "damned Confederate monuments."

Eventually, Mom got up the courage to go home to visit. By then, she was pregnant and smoking cigarettes, a habit that persisted for the rest of her life and that would eventually claim her life at 68. Mom came home with her beau, a young man wearing his hair "conked" (chemically straightened). Such were the times that men, as they used to say, did "the right thing" if they impregnated a woman. Mom and Dad married in Maryland in 1945. I was born that next spring. Mom was 19. Daddy was 22. The union lasted until Daddy died in 1983.

She and Daddy welcomed a second daughter, Deborah, in 1953, and a third, Georgeann, in 1955. My family was poor, but I don't recall ever going hungry because we had nothing to eat. In fact, I really was proud to have my mom and dad living under one roof. I overheard arguments every now and then, but my father never raised his hand to my mother or called her names. When some people made fun of my father because he would get drunk and stumble home, my favorite response was, "At least, I've got a father, and everybody in my house has the same last name!"

I've never had children and by my best reckoning, I literally willed myself not to because of my real fear of giving birth and the possibility, of having to raise a child alone.

It happens all the time. People fall in love, they get married, they get pregnant, have a baby, and after a while, somebody wants out, and somebody, usually the woman, becomes the primary caretaker. For me, divorce isn't the worst of it. The worst of it would have been having a lifelong connection through the child to someone I had stopped loving or simply couldn't bear to be around. I had no desire to be miserably tethered to someone just for the sake of a child. I'm not that good of an actress to be able to hide my negative feelings for very long. Even when I choose to be silent, my face tells it all.

David's son shared with me that before his father became really ill, they had a heart-to-heart. He asked his father why he did some of the things that he did, and especially why David wasn't there for him at important times in his life. While he learned some things about life from his dad, Levet said it was his step-father who taught him the most about how to be a good man, a present father and faithful husband and provider.

It was a tough conversation during which David said to Levet, "Son, I love you, but I was always where I wanted to be." I'm sure that wasn't the response that Levet wanted or expected, but he accepted his father's explanation as typical of who David was. Like it or not, David was being his authentic self. Levet could have been bitter about his father's failings, but when his dad needed him most, Levet didn't hesitate to step up. What I saw between them when I came along was a warm relationship. I always enjoyed hearing those two laughing together and debating which of them was the best cook. David was very proud of what his son had accomplished. Levet had a good job, a beautiful family and a lovely home.

When David came to Louisville, we talked a lot about our lives over the years since we had last seen each other. I told him some of the twists and turns that my life had taken after I moved out of the projects. I had been a secretary. I took up smoking, but never drinking or drugging. I always seemed to be in the right places at the right times. In the late 1960s through 1970s, I found myself in the throes of the black cultural renaissance in Harlem. I dabbled with acting as a member of the National Black Theater. It was an amazing time to be young, gifted and black. I compared it to the Harlem Renaissance in the 1920s and 1930s when Langston Hughes, Zora Neale Hurston, Wallace Thurman, W.E.B. DuBois and many others were waging war on Jim Crow with their poems, novels and music.

I got involved with the Civil Rights Movement, almost by accident. I was working in the national office of the Episcopal Church. I was sitting at my desk typing and could feel a thin, lanky brother with a halo Afro watching me. I kept typing, and after a while, Ralph Featherstone, sauntered over, leaned down and whispered, "We need you, Sister." Featherstone aka "Feather," a native of Washington, D.C. and an educator, was a veteran of the dangerous Mississippi and Alabama voting rights and freedom school campaigns. The "We" whom "Feather" believed needed me was the Student Nonviolent Coordinating Committee. Pretty soon I was volunteering in SNCC's New York office, working closely with the executive secretary, the brilliant James Forman, and Irving Davis, chair of SNCC's International Affairs desk. I met Mae Jackson at the SNCC office. She's a yet unsung civil rights warrior and she's still my dear friend and she's still on the battlefield for justice.

H. Rap Brown, who succeeded Stokely Carmichael, as chairman of SNCC, and who once said, "Violence is as American as cherry pie," was in and out of the New York office. I never had much conversation with Rap because, to be honest, I was intimidated by the sheer force of his personality. I was awe of Rap's brilliance and his ability to turn a phrase.

The people who really frightened me were the Black Panthers who came through the SNCC office during a short-lived alliance between the two organizations. I never will forget the day that Bobby Seale came to the office to meet with Forman. I was in a back office when one of Seale's underlings came back, spun me around in my secretary chair and demanded that I stand up for the chairman. I stood, and Seale looked me up and down but said nothing. Now, that was scary, and the clash of cultures between SNCC and the Panthers was obvious to me. Both organizations had their sexist elements, of course, but looking back, from my female perspective, the difference was between men who asked for what they wanted and men who were in the habit of taking what they wanted. The Panther men were takers, or so it seems to me from what I've read and heard from former Panthers.

Sadly, in March 1970, Feather and William "Che" Payne, a SNCC organizer, were killed instantly by an explosive device that went off in a car in which they were passengers. The authorities said Feather and Che were on their way to Bel Air, Maryland, to blow up the courthouse where Rap was supposed to go on trial for arson and incitement to riot. He was charged after violence and fires erupted following a speech he delivered in Cambridge, Maryland. SNCC said the explosion was murder with the intent to disrupt the Black Power Movement.

The violent deaths of my friends weren't the only reminders that being involved in the Civil Rights Movement was hazardous to one's health and livelihood. Two FBI agents actually showed up at my job to question me about Rap's whereabouts after he failed to show up for one of his trials. I didn't know anything, but learned that low-hanging fruit like me was not exempt from FBI Director J. Edgar Hoover's efforts to discredit civil rights activists and organizations.

Around this time, I met Gerterlyn O. Dozier, Lyn to her friends, whose initials spell GOD. Lyn pushed and prodded me to go to college, and hung with me every step of that journey, from the bachelor's degree I earned with honors from Hunter College to the master's I received from Columbia University's Graduate School of Journalism in 1980, 17 years after I graduated from high school.

If I had a million tongues, I could not begin to thank all my mentors. I cannot even name all of them because many were mentoring me when I didn't realize what they were doing. I didn't recognize that, ever so gently, these men and women were nudging me to strive to become my best self. When I think about my mentors, and the list is long, I am reminded of 1 Corinthians 13:11 (KJV) which says, "When I was a child, I spake as a child, I understood as a child, I thought as a child: but when I became a (wo)man, I put away childish things."

Lyn is the mentor that helped to prepare me for the other mentors and the experiences that would come later. We met while working together for the national Episcopal Church's General Convention Special Program in New York. She was a GCSP executive and I was a secretary. Despite our different professional ranks and age differences (she's 13 years older), Lyn and I bonded. I can't recall what we were talking about, but one day, with nary trace of a smile, Lyn looked at me and said, "When you grow up, you're going to be a helluva woman." I took offense and quickly fired back. "I *am* grown!"

I was immature and mouthy, but Lyn didn't hold that against me. She saw something in me and kept encouraging me to go to college, which I finally did in 1972, because she said, "You are smart, and you always have something to say, even if you don't what you're talking about."

She let me read out of her personal library and bought me books to start my own. We patronized books stores like Lewis Michaux's National Memorial African Bookstore on 125th Street. Lyn took me to meetings, lectures and social gatherings all over Harlem and introduced me to many of her friends, including Betty Shabazz, Malcolm X's widow, and Barbara Sizemore, the first African American woman to lead a public school system in a major city, Washington D.C., as well as John Henrik Clarke, a historian, writer, and teacher. He was among the pioneers who fought to get Africana and Pan African Studies included in college curricula.

Lyn was active in the African Heritage Studies Association, a collective of Afrocentric scholars who in 1969 set out to teach and preserve the history and contributions to the world made by Africans on the continent and in the diaspora. I accompanied Lyn to AHSA book discussions and signings for many important writers. I was mesmerized listening to Ivan Van Sertima, the historian and author of several books, most notably, "They Came Before Columbus: The African Presence in Ancient America."

With Lyn, I had several occasions to be in the company of Yosef Alfredo Ben-Jochannan, affectionately known as "Dr. Ben." He had a great sense of humor but was deadly serious in his opposition to the "Europeanized" versions of African History. Dr. Ben lectured widely in America and abroad and did extensive research that yielded several books, including "Black Man of the Nile and His Family."

I met Alex Haley at an AHSA book party. Haley, a journalist noted for his books, "The Autobiography of Malcolm X" and "Roots: The Saga of an American Family," was a masterful storyteller. I couldn't have imagined that 16 years after meeting him that I would spend a weekend interviewing and hanging out with Haley at his farm in Tennessee. *Essence* commissioned me to write the piece, which ironically was published in the February 1992 issue, the month that Alex Haley died at age 70.

Lyn also taught me how to drive, saying, "You need to be able to leave a party when you want to." She took me to see my first Broadway play, the 1970 musical, "Two by Two" starring Danny Kaye. I recall being more enthralled by the set design than the singing. At some point, Lyn said that I needed to travel more. She helped to finance my first trip to Europe in 1976. I went to Paris alone. As a New Yorker, I had no trouble navigating the Paris Metro, and I used discount coupons to be able to afford admission to the famous sites— the Eiffel Tower, the Rodin Museum, the Palace of Versailles, and the Louvre — and to take the boat ride down the Seine. I visited the site where Josephine Baker, the African American dancer and singer, performed in the 1920s and 1930s. Disgusted by American racism, Baker became a French citizen and worked for the resistance when the Nazis occupied France during World War II. Because my budget was tight, I ate a lot of bread and cheese during my trip, but I splurged to pay a street artist in Montmartre to do a charcoal portrait of me. It wasn't very good. I have Lyn Dozier to thank for encouraging me to go to college and travel widely, sticking with me every step of the way and raising my political and social awareness.

David seemed to be both impressed and fascinated by the roads I'd traveled during the decades since last we'd seen one another, After many years of flying solo, I felt there was something special about David and I imagined myself coming in for a landing with him. Maybe I could trust him with my heart. What did I have to lose? What did David have to lose? What did we have to lose? We weren't so young anymore. Before David's visit to Louisville ended, the magic words flew out of my mouth, "Come live with me." I figured that we could spend the rest of our days sharing our stories, enjoying David's cooking, going to parties, traveling and dancing in the living room. As my second husband, Karamoko Bayé, who gave me my beautiful last name, often said, "If it doesn't cost you your life, it's not the worst thing to ever happen to you."

Speaking of Karamoko, I met him in 1977. He swept into my life like a whirlwind, utterly brilliant and cocksure. I was still completing my undergraduate degree and working part time for Dr. Lucius Walker in the National Council of Churches' Office of Church and Society. Karamoko eyed me on his way into a meeting with Lu and when the meeting ended, he invited me to lunch. I was curious about the tall, thin, good-looking stranger.

Over lunch, "K" dazzled me with his vocabulary and his talk of the work he was doing for prison reform. He was on the board of the Center for Constitutional Rights, which then and now is dedicated to "the creative use of law as a positive force for social change." K was executive director of PACE, Prisoners Accelerated Creative Exposure, the non-profit that he founded to advocate for imprisoned artists. His advisory board included Bill Kunstler, the famed civil rights attorney, and Dick Gregory, well known for his comedy, but better known for his activism and biting analyses of American racism.

By the time I met Karamoko, he had a published novel, "A Right to Anger," and he was a darling of many white leftists. He was much in demand as a speaker, and with PACE as his vehicle, he traveled the country and abroad talking about prison reform and hosting art exhibitions to sell the work of the artists he represented.

K had all the right stuff for the young woman that I was at that time.

In June 1978, about a year after we met, Karamoko, aka Antonio Roberto Fernandez, and I were married in the rear garden of a black-owned art gallery in New Orleans's French Quarter. My friend Phillip Baptiste, executive director of that city's Opportunities Industrialization Center Inc., gave me away. I met Phillip in the early 1970s when I worked for OIC New York. Phillip's lady friend at the time, whose name escapes me, stood as my maid of honor. Another dear friend, the late, great storyteller and actor John O'Neal, a co-founder of the Free Southern Theater, wrote and performed a special piece for the occasion. Akinshiju Ola, a freelance photographer, journalist and New Orleans native, was Karamoko's best man.

Karamoko and Akinshiju met when they were inmates at the then-notorious Marion Federal Penitentiary in Illinois. Karamoko was serving time for bank robbery. I never knew why Akinshiju was incarcerated, and I learned pretty quickly that it was best not to ask.

In any event, Karamoko, Akinshiju and their comrades were leaders of Marion's Black Cultural Society and wrote book reviews and articles about the black diaspora for the society's Black Pride Newsletter. They wrote and read deeply and were inspired by Malcolm X; Karl Marx; and Franz Fanon, the psychiatrist from Martinique, beloved by African American activists for his cogent analyses of the impact of colonization on the colonized in his books, "Black Skin, White Masks," and "The Wretched of the Earth." They also studied the life of Amilcar Cabral, the brilliant engineer, poet and, anti-colonist leader from Guinea-Bissau, whose advocacy of African liberation, ended with his assassination in 1973. "K" had a beautiful voice and besides proposing to me, one of the most romantic things he did was to sing to me in public. We'd stopped in the old Showman's Lounge on 125th Street next door to the Apollo Theater and were sitting a table talking when out of the blue, K stood up, dedicated and then sang "My Funny Valentine" to me. I basked in the glow of his attention and the approving nods of the strangers in the bar who clapped after K's impromptu performance.

Karamoko was one of the most charismatic men I'd ever encountered, and for a while our marriage worked, but about four years in I realized that though he had the intellect and the gift of gab, he lacked the spiritual and emotional warmth that I craved. I believe K loved me in his own kind of way, but eventually we grew apart. We inhabited the same physical space, but we were living separate lives. In the early 1980s, my father had been diagnosed with lung cancer. My marriage just wasn't my priority. My father was. I was also writing my novel, "The Africans," which was published in 1983 and Karamoko was busy with his various activities and traveling.

Meanwhile, I was increasingly unnerved K's shifting moods. For example, I accompanied him on one of his speaking engagements. We were staying at a rustic resort in New Hampshire's White Mountains. After the speech, I went back to our cabin. K didn't come back for a long time. When I asked where he had been, he hauled off and slapped my face so hard it stung. He apologized profusely and promised it would never happen again. We left in the middle of the night without saying so long to our hosts. I was eager to get back to New York. We didn't break up immediately, but I was done. After a while, K moved out. Where to I did not know and did not ask. We talked on the phone periodically.

Months later, we agreed to have dinner and talk. We went to *Under the Stairs*, one of our favorite restaurants on the West Side. He hinted that maybe we should try getting back together, but I was saying, "Not so fast." I needed to tell him how much he had hurt and disappointed me. He wasn't trying to hear me, so I picked up my purse, he picked up his briefcase and we left. The last time that I saw Karamoko Bayé was in my rear-view mirror when I drove away.

He still called from time to time but never said, and I didn't ask, what he was into. Then in 1982, or early 1983, a friend called and said that K had supposedly gone to a meeting in Detroit and didn't come back. Weeks, months and then years passed. Karamoko had vanished like a ghost. His disappearance was so mysterious that my father, sick as he was, begged me not to go looking for "K," so I didn't. I've written more about Karamoko than I intended, but he was an important part of my life. I loved him when I loved him. I learned a lot from him. Whatever he got into after we broke up, he kept it away from me.

Moving to Louisville in 1984 provided much needed physical and emotional distance from the break-up with Karamoko and his subsequent disappearance. I arrived in a new city with a great job, fully prepared to start from scratch. My heart was open and over the next 30 years, I dated and secretly crushed on a few men, but I count only two relationships that I consider fairly serious.

I met Charles Douglas about a year after I moved to Louisville. He was nine years older and one of the kindest and gentlest souls I've ever encountered. If I required nothing more than to be taken care of, Charles was that man. Not that I was eager to marry again but Charles had been terribly scarred by a marriage that ended years before we met. As wonderful as he was, he couldn't give himself to me as fully as I needed him to, and so after two and a half lovely years as a couple, I pulled away. We never argued and true to his nature, Charles remained in my life as a friend. We went on dates from time to time and if ever something needed fixing at my place, Charles came to the rescue with toolbox in hand. It broke my heart when I learned that Charles, a Navy veteran was in the Veterans Hospital suffering with dementia. On one visit I asked him, "Do you know who I am?" Flashing his familiar sweet smile, he replied, "Sure I do." I could see him struggling, but he couldn't pull my name from his memory. Charles died in August 2018. A kinder, gentler man I may never meet again.

My other serious relationship was with Everett Todd. I met him in 1991, shortly after completing my Nieman Fellowship for Mid-Career Journalists at Harvard University. From the beginning, I was more smitten with Everett than vice-versa. He is good-looking, but my real attraction was that he is smart and multi-talented. However, and I've told him this, many times, that his blessings are also his curse. Everett is so smart and so good at so many things that he can't settle down and focus on any one thing for very long. He's a complicated man and I wasn't emotionally equipped to deal with all that he had going on. He proposed twice and likely would have married me had I agreed, but I knew deep down that marriage wouldn't have worked for us.

Even so, our relationship dragged on for more than a year, because I came to love his family, and when he wanted to be, Everett was fun to be around. Yet, he would pull disappearing acts and then resurface. Finally, he announced that he was in another relationship. I wasn't shocked and to be honest, I was quietly relieved. And, as seems to be my pattern, Everett rotated to the friend zone where he remains to this day.

After Everett, I dated but didn't emotionally invest in those relationships and so when they petered out after a few weeks or months, my attitude was, "Such is life." I had experienced too much, observed too much, heard too much, and knew too much about relationships to believe that it is always necessary to be in one. Marriage isn't for everybody. I don't sit around fretting about it. I've been married twice, and I've been single more years than married, but I'm not burned out on love.

I stayed busy and my life was so full that when David re-emerged, I was caught off guard by how quickly he beat a path into my life and into my heart. Growing up in the same places at roughly the same times, of course, played a big part, but during that weekend in Maryland, David awakened feelings that I guess I had shoved onto a back burner. When he played our music, looked at me, danced with me, talked with me, listened to me and held me in that special way, it felt so real, so authentic, so honest and a lot of other adjectives that I couldn't resist. It felt like I needed David and that he needed me. From time to time, David and I discussed marriage. I joked that I wouldn't marry him because he had bad credit, but had he lived longer, we may have gotten married.

I can say with near certainty that had David and I met up again during his crazy years, it's highly unlikely that we would have made a serious love connection. I'm convinced that when we met again in 2010 it was when we were supposed to.

Shortly after David had returned home to Pittsburgh, a manila envelope came in the mail with a color photograph of him inside. The handsome devil was wearing a gray sports jacket, black turtle neck and the smile of a choir boy. I could see how he could be mistaken for Jim Brown, the legendary professional football player. David had the picture taken by a professional photographer and his son joked that it was his father's "campaign" photo to reel me in.

Chapter 5

I Blame You - (Ledisi)

David jumped at my offer to come live with me in Kentucky. He gave notice to his employers and informed his friends. By late October 2010, David was headed westward toward me. After many years of being a rolling stone, David was adept at traveling light. He showed up in Louisville after the six-hour drive with his 40-inch, flat-screen TV, his computer, chess set, boom box, music, a few books, family photos and clothes all packed into his car.

Even making room in my home for David's few possessions required a major adjustment. Every closet, every dresser drawer, every bookshelf, every wall and every smooth surface was filled with *my stuff*. My dishes, my coffee cups, my silverware, my pots and pans, my photo albums, my awards, my artwork, my collectibles and miscellaneous memorabilia. It was all mine, mine, mine.

Having lived alone for many years, I had to learn how to share all over again. I emptied dresser drawers and closets to make space for David's stuff. I repurposed a small patio to do double duty as the music room and David's man cave.

I was set in my ways and needless to say, David had ways of his own, but we made it work. "Moving forward" wasn't simply one of David's favorite things to say, it defined how David lived his life.

The plan was for David to get a job in Louisville, preferably managing an apartment complex. Though he had other jobs that were dear to his heart, especially working with troubled youths and the mentally challenged, the majority of David's professional experiences were in housing management and construction. He developed competence in these related fields back in the 1960s when he was a community activist in East Harlem.

As a black Puerto Rican who spoke fluent Spanish, David had access to people who traditionally had no voice, and they were more apt to trust one of their own. It didn't hurt either that the social and political consciousness of East Harlem's younger Puerto Ricans was rising. Some of the more militant brothers and sisters affiliated with the Young Lords, Puerto Rican activists who organized around the principles of self-determination and neighborhood control. They were similar in their ambitions to Huey Newton's and Bobby Seale's West Coast based Black Panther Party. The Young Lords were also surveilled by the FBI's Counterintelligence Program that was created specifically to disrupt domestic groups deemed to be extremist. Even the prince of non-violence Dr. Martin Luther King, Jr. was the object of surveillance under COINTELPRO.

David was especially proud of his time working for Hope Community in East Harlem. He had to mix it up sometimes with construction trade goons and developers to secure jobs and housing for people who lived in the neighborhood. In his position, David often supervised people who had college degrees when all he had was a G.E.D., a few college credits and certificates from training programs in the housing trade. David also had what many of those nice, better educated, do-gooders who had come to East Harlem to help didn't have: he had a "master's degree" in the streets. He knew East Harlem inside and out. He had hung out on those streets ever since childhood. He knew the number runners, the players, the whores, the pretenders, the gang members, the junkies, the con artists and some of the real mobsters who controlled the local rackets.

He knew the neighborhood stores that were fronts for the mob. The dead giveaway were the grocery stores that had mostly empty shelves and maybe a jukebox that hadn't been stocked with new music in years. The real action was in the back rooms and basements.

Rumor had it that Choo Choo's, our favorite candy store on First Avenue, was a mob front. Maybe so, but Choo Choo's display cases were always fully stocked and the music in the store's jukebox was always up to date. Whatever Choo Choo was into, David said that the candy man took a special interest in him. "Choo Choo said that I was too smart to be a knucklehead," David said. While he listened politely when Choo-Choo sought to steer him from trouble, David had to admit that he did make plenty of knuckleheaded moves.

When we were growing up in East Harlem, it wasn't unusual for adults who routinely engaged in unsavory and illegal activities, to discourage neighborhood youngsters from doing the same. If they were asked to explain the contradiction, their excuses included that they did not have much education, didn't speak good English, or didn't have better options when they were kids. I remember hard-core junkies with festering sores from injecting heroin, needle tracks, grotesquely swollen legs and slack jaws, pointing to their sorry selves and saying, "Don't be like me. Go to school. Get an education. Be somebody. This ain't living." Seeing them day after day huddling in groups and looking like the walking dead scared me straight, but for many kids, the junkies' admonitions fell on death ears, and before long, they became drugged out zombies too.

When David moved to Louisville, I was still working at the newspaper and knew a few people that I thought would be willing to help with David's job search. I had faith that all the experiences that David brought to the table, his great personality and his fluency in Spanish would impress potential employers. I was mistaken. Some of my connections talked a good game, but no job offers materialized, and David's search on line and in traditional newspaper want ads, drew a few nibbles, but no bites. We had failed to take into account that many employers don't fall over themselves to hire 60-some-year-olds.

We were disappointed, but in retrospect, David may have been relieved. He was a big man and outwardly appeared to be robust, but even before the lung cancer diagnosis, David's health was fragile. He was a smoker and a diabetic who suffered with COPD, a pulmonary disease.

I also smoked for years. I was up to three packs a day in 1990, when thanks to a single $35 hypnosis session, I kicked my habit. Since then, I make it a point not to harass those still addicted to tobacco, but I have low tolerance for even the smell of cigarettes. I don't permit smoking in my home or in my car. Soon after David came to live with me, I encouraged him to stop smoking, and he agreed. He quit cold turkey, but his lifestyle change was too little too late.

So, David came to me not in the best of health, but he was crafty trying to hide his challenges, and he really didn't look like the sum total of his ailments. His strong will kept him moving forward.

When he claimed the kitchen as his domain, he got no argument from me, but I struggled early on with some of our differences. What I didn't know was how serious David was about us dining together. Background music was fine, but TV-watching and taking phone calls, unless there was an emergency, could wait until after our meals. I was very aware that something seemingly so trivial could be a deal breaker for me. We eventually reached a compromise. Some days, we ate David's way, together at the dining room table, and on other days, we ate my way, off snack tables in the den while watching "Jeopardy" on TV.

A long-distance romance and making promises and love talk over the phone was very different from living under one roof. My friends reminded me that relationships require compromise. You give some, and you get some. Old habits don't die easily, and especially at our ages.

After David's fruitless job search, we revised our life plan. We did the math and figured that we could maintain our modest lifestyle with the incomes we both were generating. Once we figured out that we had more than enough to cover the bills, we decided to take a trip to Puerto Rico.

We weren't loaded, but with David, I was a happier version of my old self. Many of my friends noticed that I seemed to be having the time of my life. Ed and Bernadette Hamilton noticed, and at David's memorial service four years later they delivered a joint statement that touched my heart. David connected with Ed when he spent a day at Ed's sculpture studio. At the time, Ed was working on yet another Lincoln, this one a standing 12-foot statue commissioned by Centre College in Danville, Kentucky.

As Ed recalled, he had just received an enlarged model of his statue the day that David stopped by. The model arrived in pieces — the head, the torso, the legs, the arms and the hands — that Ed had to put together and line up just right before applying the clay in preparation for the completed statue. Ed was going up and down the ladder, and he asked David to assist by handing him various parts of the statute. "He was a big help," Ed said and once he was done fitting the parts and making his adjustments, he and David stood back and looked.

Well, you couldn't tell David that he wasn't a sculptor, too. He was thrilled about his role in Ed's creation. I was thrilled that Ed, who has sculpted such important public art works as the Spirit of Freedom Memorial to the Black Civil War Veterans in Washington, D.C. and the Amistad Memorial in Connecticut, took the time to invite David into his world.

At the memorial service, Bernadette said, "Ed and I knew when David came into Betty's life. We felt her happiness. We noticed the change in her walking and the gleam and glow in her eyes when she mentioned his name. Her looking for Mr. Right had stopped."

Then Ed said, "We knew we were looking at two people who seemed to be meant for each other. What a blessing. There was love, chemistry, passion and a commitment to spend their lives together."

Chapter 6

Ain't No Stoppin' Us Now - (McFadden & Whitehead)

In the brief time we had together, David and I took plenty of photos and were truly social butterflies. We accepted almost every holiday invitation, so making the rounds provided opportunities for him to experience Louisville hospitality, to meet my friends, and for my friends finally to meet and greet the special man who had come back into my life after nearly 50 years.

David made a fine co-host for my annual New Year's Day open house. It was a tradition that I had started several years before. The open house had become a much bigger deal with many more guests, and it was much more expensive to host. What started as a gathering for a few people had morphed into a large, eclectic mix of friends and colleagues. The pious teetotalers and scholarly types mixed with the serious party people, who inevitably came late and stayed late.

David easily navigated my Louisville social circle and charmed a lot of people in the process. One minute, he would be conversing with the intellectuals, and the next minute would find him chatting with friends who didn't care about politics or scholarship. Not everyone can migrate across educational, class and racial lines, but David could. Bless his heart.

We entered 2011 "partying hearty," but had already decided to visit Puerto Rico. It was a fortuitous choice as that turned out to be David's final visit to the birthplace of his parents and grandparents.

Puerto Rico, here comes Moodles and Moo Moo! We landed in San Juan, picked up our rental car and drove to Courtyard by Marriott Isla Verde Beach Resort. We were giddy when we bopped into the lobby to check in. Our smiles turned to frowns in short order when we learned that the resort had tacked on unadvertised extra fees.

"Talk to your people, 'cause I'm not having it," I said. In no time flat, David took over. He started talking in Spanish to the desk clerk and gesturing toward me as I sat a short distance away fuming. I couldn't understand what all he was saying in Spanish, but I did hear David say loud and clear in English, "She's not going for this, so I think you better fix it." A manager appeared, offering apologies for the "misunderstanding," and next thing I knew the hotel waived the fees, and a bellman escorted us to an upgraded room with an ocean view on a higher floor. When the bellman left, we closed the door and laughed at our good fortune.

I'm thoroughly convinced that the situation might not have ended on such a happy note had David not played what I jokingly refer to as his *mi hermano* card. What I noticed from my experiences with David is that despite differing accents and certain words having different meanings, Spanish-speakers, no matter their national origins, always seem to search for ways to communicate and even to go the extra mile for one of their own. David definitely was part of the Afro Latino diaspora.

We unpacked, turned on the radio and opened the doors to our balcony with the ocean view to let in the sweet tropical breeze. Later, as the sun began to set, we mellowed out listening to the mating calls of the Puerto Rican coquí frog. "*Ko-Kee! Ko-kee,*" the males croak. David poured himself a stiff drink, lit up a cigarette and kicked back like he was king of the world. David was *home.*

He told me all kinds of stories about his time living and working in Puerto Rico. He apparently had an extended beach bum period. He and his buddy Melé chased women and caught crabs or fish to cook over a fire on the beach. Sometimes they would lie under the stars smoking reefers and talking trash. David had hoped to see Melé during our visit, but we heard that he had moved to Vieques, an island off the shore of Puerto Rico. Unfortunately, that island wasn't on our itinerary.

We deliberately skipped hotel food. David wanted authentic cuisine and got all excited one evening when he spied a sign outside a restaurant not far from our hotel advertising *mofongo*. The soupy, mashed green plantain dish is spiced up with olive oil, garlic and bacon served over chicken, fish or shrimp. My baby was about three mouthfuls into his meal when he scrunched up his face and declared the *mofongo* subpar. He couldn't seem to comprehend how any self-respecting restaurant, in Puerto Rico no less, couldn't properly prepare something that's virtually a national dish. We eventually found a restaurant that came closer to serving the kind of *mofongo* David had grown up eating in his mother's kitchen. The restaurant was tucked inside a small mall along *Isla Verde's* hotel strip. The food was priced well, and we ate there at least three times. That restaurant stayed crowded, but the one that served bad *mofongo* was mostly empty whenever we passed by. I had been to Puerto Rico several times, but it was a very different experience being there with my man, who just so happened to speak the language and also knew the island's backroads, as well as its main drags.

I had my first encounter with Jealous David in Puerto Rico. One day, I was sitting by the hotel pool just chilling under the rays of the Caribbean sun when an uninvited, handsome gentleman, wearing a suit, sat on the lounger next to mine and struck up a conversation. He said that he was on a break from a meeting of Walgreens Pharmacy managers being held at our hotel. He said he was a regional manager overseeing several stores on the island. The guy was a little full of himself, but I didn't get the feeling that he was coming on to me.

Suddenly, like an apparition, David stepped out from behind the hedge encircling the pool. He was not smiling. I introduced him as my husband. David apparently had seen the man hand me one of his business cards because, without missing a beat, David whipped out his wallet and handed the man one of his business cards. It was awkward, and the gentleman took that as his cue to move on. David snarled. He dismissed the stranger's story about his high position with Walgreens. That's the sort of game local players run on unsuspecting tourists, David insisted. He was over-reacting, but my ego did get a nice jolt at the idea that my honey bunny believed that, flabby thighs notwithstanding, I looked good enough for a stranger to hit on. "Go, Betty!"

David was a strong swimmer, but his best efforts notwithstanding, he couldn't teach me. Nobody could. More than anything, David yearned to swim again in the ocean, although a swimming pool would suffice if that was all that was available. One afternoon, I sat dry docked on the hotel beach while David slow jogged into the water. He was in his element. He swam far out, but I could keep my eyes on him from where I sat. I waved at him and he waved back.

I turned my attention away at some point, and when I looked up again, I couldn't see a bobbing head. David had disappeared. I looked, and I looked and then I panicked. I ran down toward the water calling his name. If he was really in trouble, I couldn't jump in to save him. I was about to summon the lifeguard when I spied David again, still far out, going up and down in the water, but farther down the beach. I signaled him to get back to the beach so that I could take my heart out of my mouth and curse him out for scaring me. When he finally did swim back, I was so relieved that I forgot to be angry.

David explained that the current was strong and that he knew better than to swim against it. So, he stayed with it as it moved him, not further out to sea as it seemed from my vantage point, but sideways down the beach.

A few days later at Luquillo Beach, the Puerto Rican Riviera some call it, David had a real panic attack in the ocean, and rightly so. He was up to his neck in the water. I was watching him, and it seemed from my vantage point that he was frozen in one spot. What was he doing? I thought. He wasn't swimming. He wasn't laughing or waving. He was just standing there. I didn't panic, however. I figured that David was just waiting for the right moment to swim back to shore. After a while, he did. He didn't say anything, but immediately rummaged through our beach bag to retrieve one of his inhalers. He took a couple puffs, and after a while, he relaxed. When he finally did speak, David said that he stood still in the water because he was struggling to catch his breath and feared that he wouldn't have the energy to swim back. He was really shaken up. He didn't get back in the water for the rest of that day.

As if that wasn't enough drama for our day at Luquillo, we would have another scare later that afternoon. We were heading back to our car. David was walking ahead of me, so he didn't notice when I tripped over a raised metal platform on the beach that was partially hidden by sand. It may have been a utility cover. Whatever it was, I went down hard. David turned around when he saw a bunch of people running in the direction from which we had come. People were standing over me and speaking in Spanish. Their voices seemed to be coming from far away. I must have had the wind knocked out of me because when I finally focused, I saw David's face. He was scared. I heard someone suggest transporting me to the hospital, but I wasn't bleeding, so I declined medical treatment. I wasn't about to spend a moment of my precious vacation in an emergency room. David helped me to my feet. I was light-headed. The crowd dispersed, and David and I made it back to our rental car. That was a rough day, a not-so-gentle reminder that, though David and I were young at heart, we weren't kids anymore. We were more vulnerable to circumstances beyond our control like tripping, falling or finding it difficult to breathe.

It wasn't all harrowing for us two senior kids. We did the usual tourist things. We window-shopped in Old San Juan, visited a museum and took a lot of pictures. San Juan's streets are narrow, and construction projects and street repairs worsened the bumper-to-bumper traffic. David and I didn't mind sitting in traffic because we were in no rush to get anywhere by any particular time.

One day on our vacation, we got in the car and headed away from the congested tourist area in the direction of the municipality of Carolina. It was a straight shot from our hotel. After a few miles, we came upon small shacks, food stands and natural beaches. We stopped for David to buy a jug of mavi, a root beer-like drink made with tree bark and spices, from a roadside vendor. We eventually pulled the car onto a soft shoulder, took off our shoes and walked together toward the ocean. We dug our toes into the sand. We were having a grand old time, just us two, Moodles and Moo Moo, in paradise. That drive through Carolina was a great day, but the sweetest day of our vacation was the one when David and I drove for about an hour from our hotel to Humacao. His mother was born there in 1913, and it was to Humacao where David's parents retired after all their children were grown.

David's parents' house is small and sits on a narrow, dusty street in a residential neighborhood. David's older brother Ibon and his wife, Lillian, were living in the house when we came to visit. Millie, David's youngest sister, said that their father had gotten it into his head that one day his New York born and bred children would come to live in Puerto Rico permanently, and so he added a second story to the house to make room. David said that his father loved that house and had pressed him into service building the second story.

After David's mother, Dona Lydia, lost her battle with cancer in 1998, David's father grieved her absence. He was lonely and didn't quite know what to do with himself because his wife had spoiled him. Shortly after Mrs. Rivera died, Mr. Rivera was diagnosed with renal failure. David's sister Cookie left her family back home in New York and flew to Puerto Rico to be their Dad's caretaker and to try to persuade him to come back to the states so that his daughters could take turns caring for him, including getting him to and from his dialysis appointments. For the next few years, Mr. Rivera did come to New York, but he always insisted on going back to his home in Humacao. He was scheduled to fly to New York on July 10, 2001, but on July 4th, while undergoing dialysis, David, the elder, went into cardiac arrest. He died sometime later when fireworks were going off in New York.

"My father went out with a bang," Millie said. "I had spoken to him that morning. I asked him if he had his bag packed as he was only days away of arriving. He told me yes. I said I love you, see you soon, and he said I love you too."

On the day that David and I visited, one of David's older sisters, Lydia Anglero, and her husband, Librado, met us at the house in Humacao. Ibon relished explaining to us what he was growing in the small backyard. After a while Ibon, Lydia, Librado, David and I left the house and drove a short distance to a cemetery in another residential neighborhood in Humacao.

The cemetery's ground was soft, sandy and a little mushy on a sunny day, not unusual that close to the ocean. The grave markers are mostly white marble or limestone slabs set down into the ground. The graves are close together, and it took a while to locate David's parents' final resting place. Unfortunately, to get to them, we had to walk on top of other graves. At the gravesite, the siblings placed a vase of flowers, and Lydia said a prayer. I stepped away to give them a private moment. That's when, out the corner of my eye, I saw something climb out of a sunken grave not far from David's parents' site. The something was a huge, colorful, pre-historic looking iguana. I must have been a sight hopscotching between and over graves to get back to the front gate.

I always think of that iguana incident at the cemetery as "the Lazarus moment" of our Puerto Rican vacation. We all laughed about it later over dinner just up the road in a town called Naguabo. That's where David's maternal grandparents, Meliton Diaz Espinoza and Maria Rodriguez Sanchez, were born.

David and I learned on that Puerto Rico trip that we traveled well together.

Chapter 7

Living Just Enough for the City - (Stevie Wonder)

I wasn't aware until we reunited in 2010 that, during the 1950s — before we met in East Harlem - that David's family and mine lived on the same street and that David and I attended the same elementary school. After all, 8 million people live in New York City's five boroughs, and what a coincidence that the Rivera family lived in 121 Pitt Street and my family, the Winstons, lived, first in 60 Pitt, and then 57 Pitt Street.

"So," I said to David, "you've been stalking me all my life!"

Pitt Street, as was true of much of Manhattan's Lower East Side in the 1950s, was heavily populated by immigrants, and especially European Jews. That said, with our brown faces, David and I surely stood out among the students at P.S. 4 and among the boys and girls who played in Pitt Street Park.

I can imagine as well that the Winstons and the Riveras patronized the same peddler who slowly rolled his cart down Pitt Street screaming "Ice Man! Ice Man!" At his customers' requests, the ice man would grab his giant pick and tongs, and chip off large chunks of ice for the "cold closets," also known as ice boxes, where many Pitt Street families kept their food. The non-mechanical ice boxes were used by families unable to afford refrigerators or the electricity needed to keep them running.

My family had an ice box.

Maybe the Riveras and the Winstons bought fruit and vegetables from Maxie, the Jewish grocer, who operated his store out of a basement on our block.

It's possible that David's parents and mine stood next to one another making selections from the crates of live chickens that were sold on Pitt Street beneath the Williamsburg Bridge. Times were hard so chicken feet soup was on the menu for many families in the neighborhood.

The sounds of hundreds of clucking chickens and their stench permeated the air for blocks, and passersby had to take care not to slip and fall onto the chicken blood and feathers that made the sidewalks slimy.

Many families on Pitt Street shared living quarters.

My father, mother, little sister Debbie and I, moved into 57 Pitt Street with Uncle Gerald, my father's brother, and his family after my Dad "sold" our apartment in 60 Pitt to a Puerto Rican family. That was rather cheeky because we didn't own the apartment in the first place. Nevertheless, the Puerto Rican family moved into our top-floor walkup in 60 and the four of us moved across the street. Nine or 10 people inhabiting three rooms was over-crowding on steroids.

We had plenty of other relatives and extended family also living on our block. My mother's sisters, Aunt Catherine and Aunt Bernice; their husbands, Uncle Artie and Uncle Freddy, respectively, and their children, lived in 60 Pitt. My godmother, Sarah Pinder, lived in 60. Uncle Gerald's wife, Alice, aka "Sister," also had siblings who lived on the block, and Ethel McCoy, my sister's godmother, lived in 57 Pitt Street.

Similarly, David told me that his grandfather, older brothers and sisters, their spouses, cousins and sometimes close friends, lived off and on in his family's apartment down the street.

When I say that Pitt Street was a slum, I'm not overstating the case.

The five- and six-story walk up tenement buildings that we called home dated to the 1800s, and they were barely maintained by the janitors, referred to as superintendents, who often lived in the buildings in exchange for free rent.

Rats feasted and grew fat off the garbage that some people, too lazy to walk their trash down five or six flights of stairs to the garbage cans, "Airmailed" out their windows and down into the narrow spaces that separated one building from another.

Perhaps some Pitt Street tenements had bathrooms inside the apartments, but that wasn't the case in 57, where my family lived. There were two toilets per floor in the public hallways that were supposed to be shared by the four families on each floor.

The unheated hallway toilets were urban outhouses. They were nasty and they stunk, so most families only used them to dump into the toilets the contents of the "slop buckets" that they kept and used inside their apartments. As a result, even the most meticulous housekeepers were challenged to ameliorate the malodorous aromas that emanated from the hallway toilets.

Meanwhile, bathtubs, in a typical Pitt Street tenement, were located in the kitchen so many families covered their tubs with removable porcelain enamel tops that they also used as food prep stations. Since the tenement tubs weren't walled or curtained off, privacy to take a bath, was a luxury

Of course, for us kids, slum life was all we knew, and so we happily played in dirty hallways, ran up and down dirty staircases, and sat on filthy stoops and garbage tops eating candy and ice cream, blissfully unaware that our health and our very lives were in constant danger.

Yet, for all that was awful about Pitt Street, I feel fortunate, privileged, in fact, to have grown up in a place that prepared me, and David as well, to navigate racially, ethnically, and religiously diverse spaces. We lived among people who spoke little or no English, and we were exposed to all kinds of cuisine.

If we could have peeked into our neighbors' kitchens on the block, one might have witnessed a German family enjoying wiener schnitzels; a Puerto Rican family chowing down on arroz con gandules (rice, pigeon peas and pork); a Jewish family delighting over plates and bowls of gefilte fish and chicken soup with matzo balls; an Italian grandmother tasting and giving a nod of approval to her special pasta dish; or an African American family praying grace over a Sunday meal of fried chicken, yams, collard greens and cornbread.

Meanwhile, the immigrants and the migrants of Pitt and the surrounding streets and avenues, really valued education. Education was the down payment on their children's futures. They fiercely embraced the American dream that the next generation would grow up and be more prosperous than they were.

By whatever means — ship, plane, automobile, train or Greyhound bus — they had arrived on the Lower Eastside, the men and women of Pitt Street were strivers. They all had run away from something: poverty, persecution, oppression, racism, segregation or Nazis. All had left behind loved ones and familiar places to take a chance on the unknown.

As Emma Lazarus' poem, "New Colossus," that's etched on the pedestal of the Statue of Liberty in New York Harbor says, the men and women of Pitt Street, were "yearning to breathe free."

I made my first best friend on Pitt Street. She was a Jewish girl named Deborah, whose name in Hebrew means "bee." Deborah, my little friend's namesake, is recorded in the Old Testament as a prophetess, the only female judge named in the Bible, and the Israelite woman who inspired her people's military victory over their Canaanite oppressors who occupied the Israelites' Promised Land.

I loved my little friend Deborah so much that I pleaded with my mother, who was expecting, that if the baby was a girl, we would name her Deborah. My sister, Deborah, was born in 1953, and like the biblical Deborah, she's busy as a bee and will sting if you get on her bad side.

Meanwhile, my best friend Deborah taught me how to skate, allowed me play with her toys, and to watch TV with her on her family's set. We loved cartoons and *The Merry Mailman*, a children's show that ran in New York City for several years. Ray Heatherton was the mailman, and he would sing for his fans, "I am the Merry Mailman. Ring, ding, your bell will ring. That's my very special ring."

Many years passed before I understood the significance of the tattooed numbers on Deborah's mother's arm. She was a survivor of one of Adolph Hitler's concentration camps, where it's estimated that 6 million European Jews and other "undesirables" were exterminated.

I've often wondered over the years what became of my first best friend, whose last name is lost to memory, and I've wondered as well, if she ever wonders whatever became of me.

Pitt was a street of dreams for its inhabitants.

When I was very young, I was given the nickname Nooksee, reportedly because that's what I said rather than "look and see." An elderly Jewish neighbor apparently had trouble pronouncing Nooksee, and so whenever she saw me playing the hallway or outside our building, she would call me, "Ritzy, Ritzy." My father said that on Shabbat, the old lady's Sabbath day, she would offer him and other non-Jewish neighbors a few pennies to light her stove and turn her lights on so that she wouldn't break the rules of her faith.

Shortly after Christmas of 1954, our apartment in 57 Pitt burned.

A couple of my younger cousins were reportedly looking for candy in a dresser drawer and came across matches instead. I heard the fire engines from my 4th grade classroom just down the street, but didn't know that it was our apartment that burned until after school.

Tenement fires were fairly common in those ragged old buildings, and, of course, there were no sprinkler systems.

When I got home from school, my little sister was propped atop a garbage can lid looking pitiful and scared. My mother was upset about losing important documents and irreplaceable family photos. Fortunately, there was no loss of life, but the fire left my family temporarily homeless.

Cary and Anna Mae Tyler, who lived in 60 Pitt, and had five or six children of their own, took us in. In the meantime, Rev. Kilmer Myers, rector of St. Augustine, the Episcopal church on Henry Street, where we were members and I was baptized, made calls that ultimately got my family onto the emergency list for public housing.

My parents didn't want to leave the Lower Eastside, but there were no two-bedroom apartments available in any of the public housing projects in our area. My parents were given a choice of apartments in projects in the Bronx or a different part of Manhattan. Mom and Dad chose East Harlem, and in early 1955, the Winstons moved uptown, and said so long to Pitt Street.

Chapter 8

Over the Rainbow - (Patti LaBelle)

When the Winstons moved into 402 E. 105th Street in the East River Houses in early 1955, we might as well have relocated to somewhere over the rainbow.

East Harlem had a very different vibe from the Lower East Side. Both neighborhoods were ethnically diverse, but East Harlem had a different mix of nationalities and the highest concentration of public housing projects in New York City. While East Harlem had Jewish families, too, it was home to many more Irish, Italians, Germans. Plus, so many Puerto Ricans had moved into the neighborhood during the 1940s and 1950s, it was also known as Spanish Harlem or El Barrio, Spanish for "the neighborhood." New York's first "Little Italy" was also in East Harlem. I went to high school in Little Italy on 116th Street and Pleasant Avenue. During spring and summer weekends, streets in East Harlem often were barricaded to accommodate ethnic and religious parades, festivals and block parties. The sponsors often contracted carnival games and amusement park rides, everything from bumper cars to Ferris wheels

East Harlem was an exciting place when David and I were growing up there. Music was everywhere from the storefront Pentecostal churches to the record shops and the juke boxes located in many stores where for five cents a spin, you had your pick of genre.

East Harlem was also home to mom-and-pop restaurants. The variety of cuisine was mind-blowing: We had soul food restaurants, authentic pizza parlors, Italian ice shops, delis, German bakeries and *cuchifrito* take-outs, which specialized in Spanish fried pork dishes.

Compared to our apartment on Pitt Street, our new home in the East River projects was paradise found. East River Houses opened in 1941. Its six-, ten- and eleven-story tall buildings have 1,157 apartments spread over almost twelve acres from 102nd Street to 105th Street between First Avenue and the East River Drive.

My family had gone from roach- and rat-infested, cold-water, walk-up apartments to a two-bedroom apartment that had reliable steam heat, a small kitchen, a dining area and living room. An intercom system allowed us to screen our guests. Each floor had a garbage chute, and when the trash incinerated, the wall inside our apartment next to chute would get very hot.

The true *coup de grace* for my family was having a bathroom inside our apartment, and especially a bathtub where it was supposed to be, in the bathroom, and not in the kitchen. Besides a mirrored medicine cabinet built into the wall, our bathroom in the projects had a rack over the bathtub to dry laundry. It could be raised and lowered by a pulley attached to the wall. What a concept! We were living in "high cotton," as the old folks used to say.

All the buildings in the project had elevators, and East River Houses had its own day-care center, a public health station, a community center that offered tutoring and after-school recreation, and coin-operated laundry rooms strategically placed throughout the complex. A full-sized park was at the rear of the projects, and mini-play areas were scattered throughout. Residents also had access to Ward's Island, which connected to the projects via a walking bridge that spanned the East River at 102nd Street. Families picnicked there, and local schools held their field days on the island. Motown mogul Barry Gordy's film division transformed the Ward's Island walking bridge into the yellow brick road for "The Wiz," the $24 million 1978 re-make of "The Wizard of Oz." The Gordy version starred Diana Ross, Michael Jackson and Richard Pryor.

East River Houses had its own police force, all black, that helped to keep the peace. They knew the kids and their parents by name. One of the officers, Sonny, was the "good cop," with whom hardly anyone had a beef. Sonny had a sunny personality. He and my father became good friends. Sonny's partner, known to residents as Wyatt Earp, was a very different character.

I never knew what his parents named him or who first gave Wyatt Earp his nickname, but he lived up to it. He was every bit as tough as the old wild west lawman Wyatt Earp, who established his legend as a participant in the famous "Gunfight at the O.K. Corral in 1881 in a town called Tombstone. When East River project's Wyatt Earp ordered a crowd congregating or making a disturbance hollered, "Give me that stoop" or "Give me that bench," wise people scattered. The unwise were liable to find their heads having unpleasant conversations with Earp's billy club.

Meanwhile, residents who ran afoul of the project's rules were subject to fines or eviction. They faced a menu of fines of $1 or $2 for various infractions: riding a bike on the walkways, shooting craps in the halls or playing in the grassy areas separated from the pavement by low-rise chain fences. My family felt so safe living in the projects that on warm days we would prop our apartment door open with a big rock and leave it open all day. No one ever tried to break in.

Living in public housing, when my family moved in, was considered a privilege that could be snatched back. East River Houses was designed to be family friendly. It really was "a project," a grand experiment in how government could provide safe, clean housing and a myriad of social services to low-income families, who ideally were expected to eventually move out and up into the middle class. That upward-bound trajectory did work for many of our neighbors, especially our white neighbors. However, as Manhattan rents steadily climbed, to say nothing of northern-style housing discrimination, many others were stymied in their efforts to achieve middle-class status. As a result, many families stayed put in the projects because public housing rents were based on income and included utilities. If a breadwinner lost a job or fell ill, the rent would be reduced.

Public housing projects were plentiful in East Harlem and Harlem. Many were named after famous people: James Weldon Johnson, George Washington, George Washington Carver, Thomas Jefferson and Robert Wagner, a former mayor of New York.

David's family moved to East Harlem in 1960, five years after mine, and into the newly completed Woodrow Wilson projects across the street from the East River projects.

I didn't know David's family even though my cousin Roxie, her husband, Joe, and their daughter, Michelle, lived in David's building. I never really hung out in the Wilson, and certainly no to the degree that David hung out in my project. I learned bits and pieces about David's family after he and I reconnected. Some of the stories that David and his sisters shared about their family were hilarious, though clearly the Riveras struggled, as most families had to do in East Harlem.

David talked often about his grandfather Meliton, who refused to learn English, and who carved wooden toys for his grandchildren. He built a cart for David so he could earn money selling flavored shaved ice treats to the hot, harried and thirsty East Harlemites.

David said that his mother brought in extra cash for the family cooking for a restaurant and sometimes selling dinners out of their apartment. Milagros, David's youngest sister, told me about how their mother was contracted to make costume jewelry. Her assembly line was her daughters whose job was to glue on the glitter and fake stones. She also recalled David's beautiful voice and how he would sing to his sisters when they were little girls. "We would stay up and wait for him to come home," Milagros said. "My brother had a sweet tooth, and he always brought us candy."

If there was a giveaway somewhere in the neighborhood, David said that his mother headed to wherever the free stuff was being distributed. One day, she got word that someone was giving away lard, which she used in her cooking, so she got in a line to get some. His mother had been standing for a while, David said, when a man came over and whispered to her in Spanish, "Mommy, I think you're in the wrong line." It was true that something was being distributed, but it was neither free nor for cooking. Spanish slang for heroin is *"montega."* The word for lard is *"manteca."*

David's father, also named David, was a merchant seaman, and when he was away working, as the oldest child at home and the only boy still at home, young David assumed the role as the protector of his mother, grandfather and four younger sisters, Crimelda aka Cookie; Irene; Benigna aka Beni; and Milagros aka Millie. The family had its own rhythm when his father was away, but whenever he came home, David said that his dad resumed his role as the unquestioned head-of-household. He was the king, not David.

The passage of many years did not dim David's memory of the time that his father was home, and the son David was sticking close to his mother. At some point, David said his father playfully pushed him away from his mother, as if to reassert his authority. Sensing that little David's feelings were hurt, his mother pulled him close. She hugged him, kissed him and told his father to leave the boy alone. David said he felt better but admitted that he was still a little jealous of his father's position. He said he went into the room that he shared with his grandfather and sulked. David adored his mother. I regret never having met her.

My own mother was a force of nature. To make our apartment homey, my mother worked her magic on our four-and-a-half rooms. She put slipcovers over our second-hand furniture. She painted our walls vibrant colors. She repurposed two discarded orange crates into end tables. She painted them black, stood them upright on either side of the couch and used the divider inside the crates that once separated the fruit as a display shelf for her knickknacks. Mommy had plenty of those: elephants, tigers, black panthers, Chinese figurines and tiny plastic rickshaws. When one of her precious items broke, she would lovingly put it back together using Carnation evaporated milk as the glue.

Rather than replacing white sheer curtains that had been up for a while, my mother would fill the bathtub, pour in packets of Rit Dye and swish the sheers around in the water. Once the color was to her liking, she would let them dry and then re-hang her "new" sheers.

Mommy also couldn't abide bare walls. She created "black art" by tinting the faces of the white people in pictures she bought from second-hand stores. She bought boxes of mirror tiles, adhered them to the long wall behind the couch and instantly transformed our living room. Mom collected enough S&H green stamps to buy a glass-and-chrome bar cart. She wasn't a drinker, but she got a kick out of displaying her barware and gold-rimmed glasses. When she wanted something for us or for the house, she saved up for it. Every year, she joined the "Christmas Club" offered by the Union Settlement Credit Union. She faithfully put in a few dollars every week and drew out her little "fortune" in December.

My mom's living and interior decorating philosophy was simple: "Make it do what it do." Save a dollar today. Meanwhile, until you can afford a couch, throw big, colorful pillows on the floor. Can't afford a real dining room set? Buy a card table and folding chairs. Dress the table up with placemats, a bright-colored table cloth, and make your own centerpiece by filling a vase or pretty bowl with seasonal artificial flowers or imitation peacock feathers.

I can only imagine what my mother could have done if she had money to match her passions.

My parents must have been awfully happy in their new living quarters and more confident about the future because before the year was out, on November 22, 1955, my sister Georgeann was born.

While I attended the elementary school, P.S. 168 on 105th St., Mom enrolled my little sisters in the project's nursery school. That gave her the flexibility to earn a few dollars, and I do mean a few dollars, cleaning the homes of my father's bosses. Mom eventually was hired to assist Mrs. Sarah Walton, the nursery school's head cook.

Being a high school graduate and very good with numbers, Mommy probably could have gotten a better paying job, maybe as a bookkeeper. It was unlikely though that she could have found a job where she could walk around the corner to work, keep an eye on her little girls and bring home food for her family. We often ate for dinner what the nursery school kids had eaten for lunch.

My father worked in the Garment District in midtown Manhattan. He unloaded trucks and pushed racks of clothes from one fashion house to another through the district's narrow, traffic-congested streets. Every now and then a garment would "fall off" one the racks, get a little dirty and be deemed unsellable. Those lightly soiled clothes were sometimes given free to the employees. Daddy worked hard, and in the early 1980s, he told me, with tears in his eyes, that he never earned more than $6,000 in any given year.

One of my fondest memories of my dad was the time that he walked all the way from East Harlem to his job in midtown Manhattan so I could buy a steno pad I needed for school. The subway fare was 15 cents, the same price as the notebook.

My other sweet memory was my father riding the subway and then walking several blocks home lugging a heavy, old-fashioned manual typewriter for me. His bosses had gotten new typewriters for their office, and Daddy asked if they would give him one of the old ones for his daughter who was studying to be a secretary.

My father was that kind of man. Daddy was also the kind of man who didn't wait for the maintenance crew at the projects to do its job. He would sweep in front of our apartment door almost every day because we lived next to the incinerator and sometimes our neighbors' scraps of food and other debris didn't quite make it down into the chute. My father was a general in the "We don't want no roaches" army.

My parents continued our tradition of taking in family after we moved to East Harlem. I didn't know the details of why, of course, but Aunt Catherine and Uncle Artie lived with us in the projects for a while, as did Aunt Bernice, Uncle Freddy, their daughters, Susie and Pinkie, as well as Tisha, Pinkie's baby girl. My aunts and uncles got the little bedroom that Debbie, Georgeann and I shared. When the grownups took over our bedroom, we kids alternated sleeping on the couch, two big chairs pushed together, or on pallets of bed coverings on the floor in the living room. Our apartment was often overcrowded, but we made it work, and it was fun having some of my cousins around.

My family was one of the smaller ones living in the projects. Many of my friends had eight, nine or a dozen siblings. The White family, who lived in the building adjacent to ours, included 22 children, all from same mother and father. To accommodate the family, the housing authority knocked out walls to combine two apartments.

Since I didn't have a bunch of older brothers and sisters to help fight my battles, many were the times that I had to go to war with girls itching for a fight but who wouldn't dare take on one of the Whites, or some of the other large families like the McCulloughs, the Wilkinsons or the Bowmans.

My family had escaped the slums, but poverty was always lurking. Like many parents in the projects, mine worked hard but still struggled to keep up with our basic needs. My father's annual wages were low, but still too high for our family to qualify for public assistance or free school lunch.

We surely could have used welfare, but Daddy was both proud and cautious. "I don't want the government snooping around in my business and coming to my house looking into our closets," he often said. In later years, when my mother asked my father to join her in signing the papers for my then 16-year-old sister Georgeann to get public assistance as a single mother of a newborn, Daddy wouldn't sign. My mother signed the papers so she could get the public assistance, and she continued living at home. Daddy's distaste for government help showed up again years later when he threatened to walk out of the Social Security office, because, "He didn't like the way the woman behind the desk was talking to him," my mother said. She had to stop him from leaving.

Some of the happiest times in the Winston household were when our parents "hit the numbers," which they played daily. They usually placed their bets with the number runners who picked up the "policy slips" and delivered them to the gangsters who controlled the racket. When Mom or Dad got lucky, they would use their winnings to buy the necessities, but if they hit big, say for $500, they could afford to splurge on a luxury, such as the floor-model, hi-fi record player that looked like a credenza and was the centerpiece of our living room for many years.

Music had high priority in our house. We had a radio, a record player, but no television until I was in high school. Our black-and-white TV was second-hand. Sometimes we had to punch the cabinet to turn the TV on. When the picture or the sound went out, instead of calling a repair person, we would remove the suspect tubes from inside and take them to the drug store to test whichever one or two had died and buy the replacements. The vacuum tubes helped create the images we saw on television. If one went out, the TV didn't work.

My parents also didn't have a telephone until I graduated from high school in 1963, got a job as a secretary with the United Presbyterian Church and paid to have one installed. Anyone needing to reach us before then called a neighbor who would relay the message. It seems so Third World looking back.

People often talk about the awkwardness and angst they experienced in their adolescent years. They wince and sometimes actually shed real tears recollecting acne outbreaks, being too skinny, too fat, being bullied and not being invited to be part of the supposed in-crowd. You'll never hear such from me. Not to be a Pollyanna about it, but my growing up years were some of the best of my life.

Young people today surely would cringe at what they would perceive as the oppressive rules of my all-girls, public junior high school, Margaret Knox on 99th Street between First Avenue and the FDR Drive. We didn't wear uniforms at Margaret Knox Junior High like the students in Catholic schools, but on assembly days, we were required to wear dark skirts, white blouses and red scarves. Don't know who came up with the idea of what we would wear or the rationale, but everybody complied. White sneakers and green or blue gym suits were *de rigueur* for mandatory gym classes.

If we needed to go to the bathroom at school, we had to request a "pass" from our teachers. If we were stopped by a hall monitor on our way to the bathroom, we had to produce our hall pass, often a big block of wood with the words PASS stamped on it. At Margaret Knox, we weren't allowed to talk in the stairwells or in the lunchroom. As a result, girls often skipped lunch in school. They would go home or get sandwiches at stores in the neighborhood.

The "no-talking" rules were enforced by teachers, administrators and student monitors strategically placed throughout the school. To become a monitor required good grades, good attendance and a teacher's recommendation. I became a monitor so that I would have an excuse for talking in "no-talk" zones. Having power over other girls and in particular to write-up and turn in rule breakers was appealing as well. Some girls never had to fear being written up because either they had notorious reputations for fighting in the neighborhood, or their family members did. I knew better than to provoke them.

I was an A or B student in most subjects, so I was always assigned to one of the top three classes in every grade of junior high school. If you were in classes numbered 1, 2 or 3, for example, 7-1, 8-2 or 9-3, you were performing at or above grade level in most subjects. If you were assigned to classes with high numbers, you knew, everybody knew, that you were academically below grade level or were deemed a disciplinary problem. The higher your class numbers, the dumber you were believed to be.

We began each school day with the Pledge of the Allegiance, hands over our hearts to salute the flag. Jehovah's Witnesses were exempt, and unlike today, nobody made a fuss about the J.W. kids adhering to the practices of their faith, which bars participation in and paying homage to secular government. Back then, Catholic students attending our public schools had permission to leave school early on certain days so they could take part in religious studies at their parishes, and students of every faith loved when school was closed for the Jewish holidays. Who would be in school to teach if they didn't? Many of our teachers were Jewish.

The happiest times during our days at Margaret Knox were the mid-day recesses in the fenced-in school yard and the field trips to such places as the Hayden Planetarium, Ward's Island, the Museum of New York City on Fifth Avenue, or the Museum of Natural History to see the giant dinosaur skeletons.

Still, the best time of all at Margaret Knox was when the 3 o'clock bell rang, signaling the end of the school day. I must say, however, that the closing bell was a lot less joyous for girls who had been threatened with a beat down after school for some real or imagined insult. If you were the targeted girl, you had a couple of choices: You could hide in school with an understanding teacher until your nemesis had gone home, or you could walk out and run the gauntlet of instigators itching to see some hair-pulling, face-scratching or someone's bloomers exposed in the fight. We had no cell phones to call for reinforcements. No, once confronted, you either had to fight, talk your way out of a fight or be punked and picked on thereafter for no reason at all. I was not one to walk away from a fight.

Not being a punk was a great asset when I was growing up in East Harlem. When I was in the 4th grade at P.S. 168, up the street from our apartment, and still new to the neighborhood, a girl at school threatened to beat me up. I didn't really know her or why she wanted to fight me. I was afraid. I told my mother about the threat, and she said that she would take me to school and talk to my teachers. My father had a different idea. He told my mother, "If you go to school with her today, you'll have to go with her every day." He then proceeded to give me tips on how to defend myself.

"While she's running her mouth, just punch her right dead in the middle of her face, and you better try to knock her out because that might be your best and your last lick," Daddy said. He laughed at his own little joke, but he was as serious as a heart attack.

"Boopie Girl," he said, "you may not win every fight, and you don't have to win every fight, but you better let everybody know that you will fight. Otherwise, they'll beat you and take your lunch money every day."

So, off to school I went. I was alone until Theresa Terrell, my one and only school friend at the time, walked up and stood beside me. All of a sudden, the girl who had threatened me came walking up 104th Street with a crowd of kids and with her fighting clothes, a pair of dungarees, on top of her books. Her light skin was her claim to fame, I guessed, because she sure wasn't cute. With her clique cheering her on, she called me names and made a point to disparage my dark skin.

My father's instructions fresh in my mind, I let her talk, but I didn't give her time to change into her fighting clothes, I bopped her in the nose with all the strength I could muster. The blow caught her by surprise, and pretty soon hair was being pulled, fists were flying, faces were being scratched up, and the two of us were rolling around on the ground. The spectator kids were delighted. They formed a circle around us two combatants screaming, "Fight! Fight! Fight!"

A teacher eventually broke into the circle and pried us apart. "Why, I've never heard such language in my life," the red-faced woman said. Now, I'm not going to claim that I won my first fight in East Harlem, but just as my father predicted, I had at the very least established that the new girl was no punk and would fight back if provoked.

Mercifully, I wasn't the new girl for long.

I was outgoing and eventually made plenty of friends in the neighborhood; girls and boys, of every race, color and creed. My circle of acquaintances grew even larger once I entered Benjamin Franklin High in 1960. Franklin, which was located in East Harlem, within walking distance of East River Houses, drew students from throughout East Harlem, the South Bronx and central Harlem, which was predominately African American at that time.

But from elementary through high school, my core clique was girls who lived or hung out in "The Middle" of East River Houses. Thelma McCullough, Helen and Alice Lanausse, Marylou Thompson, Marilyn "Stinky" Wilson, Beverly Chappelle, Judy Mizell, Dolores Brown, Odell White, Saundra Bowman and I were "tighter than Dick's hatband." That's not to say that we never had disagreements. I actually came to blows with Marylou and Odell, but we always managed to squash our beefs and be friends again.

My clique survived childhood and young adulthood and middle-age pretty much intact, but as of this writing, ill health has claimed the lives of Helen, Beverly, Dolores, Marylou, Stinky and Thelma. My old friend Alice has suffered several strokes.

Growing up I never thought about who in my clique would be the first to die or in what order the rest of us would follow. Whatever paths we took later in life, what is absolutely true is that back in the day, we were typical big-city teenagers. We liked to play, we liked to party and we liked boys, even Stinky, who later openly espoused a preference for girls.

We were grown women when Stinky shared a story, apparently from early on in her coming out as a lesbian. She knocked on her mother's door, dressed in what had become her signature tomboy style: pants, a shirt, a baseball cap turned forward or backward, depending on her mood, and sneakers. "Stinky had every kind and color sneaker," my sister Debbie said.

Anyhow, according to Stinky, her mom looked through the peephole, refused to open the door and said, "I don't have a son." She said it so matter of factly that I couldn't discern how her mother's rejection impacted Stinky in real time. I did, however, challenge Stinky's insistence that she never wore a skirt. She did and I have the proof. It's a black-and-white photo, circa 1960, of the two of us leaning on a tree in the projects. We looked like two little thugs. Debbie made a copy of the picture and gave it to my old friend. She said Stinky stared at the photo for several minutes and then laughed her head off. "She still couldn't believe that it was her," my sister said.

Once Stinky came out as gay, she was all the way out. What you saw was what you got. I have no idea whether Stinky's mom ever came to terms with her daughter being unapologetically "butch," but what I do know is that when her mother fell ill, Stinky moved back home and cared for Mrs. Wilson until she died.

"Stinky was loyal to her mother until the end," Debbie said. She and my sister became close friends as a result of working together on various social and political campaigns in the old neighborhood, so Debbie was understandably in tears the day she called me in October 2016 to let me know that Stinky, her friend, and my friend, was dead. "I had just talked to her a couple of days before she died," Debbie said. "She had a bad cough and I told her that she needed to go to the hospital. That's the last time we spoke."

When I hung up, I thought about how life seemed to be so simple when I was kid, but now, the news I get from back home is often so sad. This one died. That one died. Miss so-so's grandson got shot.

While I can't say what was going on day-to-day in all my friends' homes, in my house, my life was pretty good. So, what if my wardrobe was limited to hand-me-downs and cheap dresses and shoes from the bargain stores on Third Avenue or from LaMarketa, on 116th Street and Park Avenue.

My parents didn't give me many chores to do around the house, and to be honest, I seldom volunteered to help out. When I was home, I passed my time reading, studying, listening to music and daydreaming.

I remember one occasion when I volunteered to wash the dinner dishes. My father jumped up from the table, ran over to the kitchen window, stuck his head out, looked toward the heavens, and yelled, "The sky must be falling. The sky is falling. Boopie Girl's gonna wash dishes." With my soapy wet hands, I hugged him, saying, "Oh Daddy, I know how to wash dishes." Skepticism was all over his face and he laughed so hard that he teared up. I loved it when my father would scrunch up that handsome face of his, throw his head back and laugh until it hurt.

Interestingly, it was my father who encouraged my lackadaisical attitude toward housework. He was the one who always said that I only had one job to do and it was to stay in school and get my high school diploma. With that diploma, he reckoned, I could take civil-service tests and eventually get a good government job with benefits. I was just a kid, and my Dad was already contemplating my retirement plan.

I took and passed a civil service test for a clerical job, but never actively pursued government employment, the route taken by many of my friends fresh out of high school. My father was right. Many of my friends back home have retired and are collecting fairly generous retirement and healthcare benefits from various city, state and federal government agencies. My sister Debbie, for example, retired from New York City Corrections, and her son, Roman Larry, who isn't 50 yet, has only a few years before he'll be eligible to retire from the New York City Housing Authority.

Meanwhile, my Daddy was a character. Just about everybody in East River knew Mr. Winston and the neighborhood thugs, thieves and addicts would never do him harm. Many were the evenings that my father came staggering home drunk. Rather than raising holy hell, my Mom would throw one of his arms over her shoulder and steer him into their bedroom, where he would fall onto the bed like a dropped anchor. Mom would lovingly remove his shoes and socks. While he snored, she would check his shoes and socks aware that that's where my Dad often kept a couple of dollars as his secret stash. When Daddy sobered up Mom didn't say a word. She knew he'd be too ashamed to ask what happened to the money that she could have used to buy food or put toward the rent.

My mother, meanwhile, was spectacularly good at shielding Debbie, Georgeann and me from grown folks' messes. We lived in a tough neighborhood, where there were plenty of scandalous characters; for example, the fathers who terrorized their wives and kids and women in the habit of going with, and even getting pregnant by, other women's husbands. Still, I didn't grow up feeling burdened by "all de troubles of de world." That would come later. When I was a kid, I acted like a kid, thought like a kid, and was treated like a kid.

In a righteous world, every child would be loved. I wish every little girl could be as free as I was. Even in a technological age, when children are tethered to electronic devices, I wish that at least once every little kid could play stick ball in the street, jump Double-Dutch rope or play or games such as Hopscotch, Hide-and-Seek and Hot Peas and Butter. I wish that every child could say that they've never been sexually molested or beaten half to death for eating the last piece of chicken.

Every child I grew up with was not that fortunate. I remember a day when my friends and I were buying candy at Choo Choo's on First Avenue. Dorothy, a school friend who didn't live in East River Houses, but lived in the neighborhood, shared a harrowing tale. She said that her mother's boyfriend was always trying to feel her up. Dorothy told her mom, but said, "My mother didn't believe me. She said that I was fresh." Dorothy didn't say whether he actually had sex with her, but we commiserated with our friend. We agreed that her mother's boyfriend was nasty, and we were sorry that her mother blamed her, rather than the pervert.

Unfortunately, all we had to offer were listening ears and sympathy. We were kids and didn't know what to do with the disturbing information Dorothy had just shared. Moreover, since we considered Dorothy's situation to be her secret, we agreed to keep it among ourselves. It never crossed our minds to tell our parents or report it to the police. Such were the times.

Another tragedy seared into my memory is the apartment fire on 102nd Street that claimed the lives of three of my girlfriends from the neighborhood, Bernadette, Joanne and Deanna. They were killed when explosive materials, perhaps gasoline, in the apartment below Deanna's blew up through the floor and trapped the girls,

Deanna's mother and Joanne's little nephew. The girls had gone up to Deanna's apartment after school to listen to records. Though severely burned, Bernadette hung on for a while and then she died.

My friends might be alive had they lived in the projects, rather than a raggedy old tenement, which was like the ones on Pitt Street. The projects were built with fireproof walls. Going to my friends' funerals was the hardest thing that I had to do in my life up to then. Grandparents die, and sometimes even parents die, but kids are not supposed to die.

My friends and I didn't have the best of clothes or the most expensive toys, and we certainly didn't have automobiles. If the need arose to travel miles from home, New York City had good public transportation 24/7. There are buses, the subways, Yellow Cabs, and so-called gypsy cabs when the Yellow Cab drivers didn't want to make pick-ups in the 'hood. A few of my friends had bicycles, but just about all the girls owned a pair of skates. Suitable for rolling on city streets and sidewalks, our skates were made of light-weight metal. Every pair came with a skate key that we used to adjust the skates to fit our shoe size and to clamp onto our shoes. A man named Everett Barney patented the clamp-on skates in the late 1800s.

My friends and I cruised the neighborhood on our skates. Sometimes we skated in formations like flocks of migrating birds up and down the East River Drive and across town to Central Park. When I was old enough to venture farther from home, I went to parties and met boys from other parts of East Harlem. One day, however, I strayed a bit too far. I got the brilliant idea to check out a boy named Stanley Jones, who lived in Brooklyn's notorious Marcy Houses.

Jay-Z, billionaire rapper and businessman immortalized the Marcy Houses, where he grew up, with the track "Marcy Me" on his 2017 album 4:44. Of course, Jay Z wasn't born when I hopped the subway to Brooklyn and made the mistake of asking a girl sitting on a bench if she knew Stanley Jones and where his building was.

Well, I never made it to Stanley's house because a group of Marcy girls came after me. They chased me back down into the subway. The only thing that spared me a certain beat down that day was that I ran fast enough to get through the turnstile and board a train that had just rumbled into the station. I was breathing hard and grateful when train doors closed. I could see the posse through the train window and realized that what stopped them was that they weren't about to pay the 15 cents fare just to beat my behind.

It was a territorial thing.

Though I was born in Brooklyn and had family members who lived there, they didn't live in the Marcy, so I was way out of place.

Manhattan kids and Brooklyn kids generally didn't mix well.

After my narrow escape, I stayed closer to home.

I was sitting with my girlfriends on a bench near my house the first time I laid eyes on David Rivera. He was walking through the projects as if he owned the place. We were all eyeballing him hard so I'm sure David knew that he was being checked out. He had the audacity to pay us no mind as he headed up the middle of East River to the basketball courts. I was curious and made a mental note to make a few subtle inquiries about the new boy in my hood.

I'd catch up with David at some other time. Meanwhile, my friends and I were doing our thing. We walked in groups to see first-run movies on 86th Street, or we'd ride the subway down to Times Square, where we had a choice of any of the several movie houses that lined both sides of 42nd Street.

Today, Time Square feels like an amusement park, but in the 1960s it was seedy and even dangerous and yet, we felt safe because my friends and I traveled in packs. We weren't bothered by the bums, pickpockets, fortune tellers, prostitutes, the johns and the sketchy "dirty old men" who patronized Times Square's many peep shows and porno movie houses.

"The World-Famous Apollo Theater," as the sign said, was also a frequent destination for my clique. We usually walked to 125th Street and saved the carfare to buy food. We would sit on the front row on the left-hand side of the stage so we could be close to some of the greatest black entertainers of all times. We saw Jackie Wilson, Chuck Jackson, Tommy Hunt and the Motown Review, including The Temptations, The Miracles, Marvin Gaye, Martha and The Vandellas and The Supremes, before Diana Ross was a big star. Jackie Wilson would come to the edge of the stage and fall down on his knees right in front of us and we would scream bloody murder. One time, Chuck Jackson actually laid down on the stage and allowed us to tear his sweaty shirt to shreds. I continued going to The Apollo as an adult and saw among others, James Brown, Richard Pryor, Bill Cosby, and

Nina Simone, who I'd never seen perform live. My excitement turned to shock when, before she sang a note, the diva got up from the piano, walked to the center of the stage, glared at the audience, and asked, "Where the hell have you all been all week?" After her tirade, she sat back down at the piano and gave her fans the performance we had expected. She was better than good.

I also saw The Jewel Box Revue at The Apollo. The revue featured 25 female impersonators, and one woman, the emcee, Storme DeLarverie, who dressed in a tuxedo and looked like a beautiful man. The review was risque´ for the times.

Beginning in the 1930s, The Apollo had been a major stop on the so-called "Chitlin' Circuit," and its stage had been crossed by just about every black entertainer of note; from Ella Fitzgerald to Aretha Franklin. But, like Harlem itself, The Apollo fell on hard times in the 1970s and 1980s. A drug epidemic ravaged the neighborhood and hundreds of once-gracious brownstones and apartment buildings were abandoned and boarded up. Harlem's nightlife took a dive as well when many of its fabled bars, nightclubs and restaurants closed their doors.

Meanwhile, with just 1,500 seats, The Apollo couldn't compete with a venue like Madison Square Garden, with 20,000 plus seats, where some of the same performers who were showcased uptown could command a lot more money. Also, by the 70s and 80s, hotels, nightclubs and the other upscale entertainment venues were booking more black acts, paying them more, and welcoming black patrons to their once segregated show rooms.

The lights never went completely out in Harlem, but they were a lot dimmer by the time I left New York in 1984. Harlem and East Harlem as well are coming back though. The boards are off many once abandoned buildings; new people and new businesses are moving in; property values are higher than ever; and The Apollo theater is being restored inside and out.

I'm an OG, as in Old Girl, and appreciate the wisdom of the songwriter who astutely observed that, "Everything must change. Nothing and no one stays the same." Yet, I'm not about to forget where I come from and I fear that it won't be long before the Harlem and East Harlem that I knew and loved will be turned into Times Square uptown, with lots of glitz and glitter, but no funk and no soul.

Chapter 9

Insanity - (Gregory Porter and Lalah Hathaway)

On June 27, 1963, my mother's birthday, I fulfilled my parents' dream when I crossed the stage of Benjamin Franklin High School to reach the waiting hands of Irving Anker, the principal, who handed me my diploma. I couldn't see him but I could hear my father hollering from the rear of the auditorium, "That's *my* daughter!" After the ceremony I ran around hugging and kissing as many of my fellow graduates as I could. I promised to keep in touch, which I have with several, but most of the boys and girls that I embraced that day I would never see again.

I was 17 years old and not exactly sure what would become of me after high school. I certainly couldn't have imagined that just weeks later, one of the girls that I hugged and kissed that day would betray the close friendship that I thought we had shared since junior high school. We fell out over a boy and never reconciled.

All these years later neither his name or her name is important. What is important is that *she* broke my heart because *she*, or so I thought, was my friend.

But here's the sweet part. She may not have intended it but her treachery fueled my decision to move out of the projects and on to a different part of town. My parents weren't pleased about me leaving home, but I had a job, thought that I was grown, and whether they admitted or not, they trusted me. What's more, my little apartment in the South Bronx was in a private home just down Croes Avenue from my cousin Pinky and her husband, Charlie Kay. I'm sure my parents told Pinky and Charles to look after me. At 17, I was hellbent and determined to be independent and to live my idealized version of being a grown up. Even my musical tastes evolved. I still loved Motown, R&B and Latin music, but I began adding jazz to my record collection. I especially loved Cannonball Adderley, Nancy Wilson, Wes Montgomery, Jimmy McGriff, Jack McDuff, Billie Holiday, Gloria Lynn and Dinah Washington, who had been one of my parents' favorite singers.

My $63 a week clerical salary went pretty far back then. It was enough to pay my expenses. But I figured I would have more fun money if I got roommate to split the $110 a month rent.

That was a good idea but I got the wrong roommate. The devil moved in with me and in no time took over. I never knew by how much, just that she older than I was. She was also bigger than me and had more life experience than me. After a while, I was so intimidated by her that I was immobilized as she exploited my space and my inexperience.

I didn't tell my parents or my cousin Pinky what was going on. I was afraid. She did all kinds of lowdown things, including having sex with her boyfriend on her side of the one bedroom that we shared while I was in the room. I was too embarrassed to get up to go the bathroom. Plus, her boyfriend was hanging out at our apartment two or three days a week and she fed him the food that she and I had purchased together to share. It was horrible.

After several months of these and other antics by that awful woman, I woke up one day and couldn't lift my arms or bend my fingers, and when I tried to walk, I couldn't. I didn't know if I was dying or what was going on. I had to call my parents. I'm not sure who gave them a ride, but they showed up about an hour later, got me dressed and took me to Metropolitan Hospital. I was admitted and the doctors poked, prodded, drew blood, took X-rays and ran all sorts of tests. They even took marrow out of my bones, and that hurt like hell. I was in the hospital for several days without a diagnosis. I called my roommate and asked her to bring my transistor radio to the hospital. She handed it to me, and for whatever reason, she went off on me and walked out. I still couldn't walk but I managed to get out of my hospital bed and crawl on my hands and knees, cussing that heifer until she got into the elevator.

How dare her have an attitude after all that she had put me through.

When my parents heard about the confrontation at the hospital, they arranged to move my belongings out of my apartment.

Once again, something bad happened that ultimately worked for my good. Just a days after the nasty verbal altercation, I was able to walk again. I could lift my arms and move my fingers. Next thing I knew, a different doctor, a psychiatrist, or maybe he was a psychologist, came and sat and talked with me for a long time. I was crying as I talked, and when I finished telling him what I'd been going through, he went away but he came back the next day. He concluded that my fear of my roommate had put me under such severe stress that my body responded by shutting down. I was also disadvantaged because I was young and had not developed the skills or the tools to fight back.

That doctor helped me to find my voice. My wretched experience living under the thumb of a bully made more real to me what my mother meant when she would say, "Self-preservation is the first law of nature."

My parents were prescient to move my stuff and discourage me from ever going back to my first apartment. We learned several months after I had vacated the premises that, during an argument, my former roommate had slit her longtime boyfriend's throat. He didn't die but it easily could have been my throat that she cut.

I had dodged a bullet that time but still had a lot to learn. I was unfocused and a bit of a mess between the ages of 17 and 21, and some of my best life lessons, I had to learn the hard way. Or, as the old folks used to say, "You pay for your learnin'" and "A hard head makes a soft behind."

At 20, I rushed into an ill-fated marriage to Brian McCrary.

After we split, I moved to the far northern part of Bronx and was befriended by a neighbor, Valarie, who was several years older than my tender 21 years. She was a barmaid and I was fascinated by her worldly ways, her beautiful clothes and lifestyle. She had a great personality, an asset given her line of work, and she got a kick out of dressing me in her furs and jewelry.

Older men who hung out in the bars loved young girls like me. They would flash their fat rolls of cash, their diamond pinkie rings and invite us to ride in their Cadillacs and Lincoln Continentals to the next club or party.

Though I never drank alcohol, I loved hanging out in bars and clubs. I'd sit at the bars, swaddled in one of Valarie's furs, people-watching, blowing smoke rings, sipping cola out of wine goblets, and listen to the music.

During my fly girl period, I lived far enough away from East River that my parents had no idea what I was up to.

Valarie took me on as her student. She introduced me to Bob. He was smooth talking like the jazz singer Billy Eckstine and bore a resemblance to Eckstine's musical protege Arthur Prysock.

Bob was more than twice my age and made his money from the illegal numbers racket. He lived in a beautiful home not far from my apartment. He had beautiful cars and lived a lush life. I was fascinated by his swag. I was working as a secretary in Harlem at the time. A couple of times a week Bob would pick me up and take me to lunch or to dinner after work. He introduced me to his friends, hustlers and politicians alike. He even took me to The Copacabana nightclub to see Bobby Darrin, who was famous for singing his big hit, "Mack the Knife." I was living a fantasy. I learned however, that Bob had a *real* girlfriend, who was his business partner. I was his toy and she didn't appear to be the least bit bothered by me.

One day, about a year into my bar fly life, I had an epiphany. I was sitting in the Club Lido on 125th Street waiting for Bob when I saw a woman sitting at the other end of the bar. Her make-up was runny and her wig was slightly askew. She was drinking brown liquor and conversing with the bartender. She wasn't bad looking, but clearly, at least it seemed to me, she'd been running around the track for a while and the fast life had taken its toll. I kept watching the woman and thinking that I could be her in another 10 or 15 years, sitting around waiting for someone to buy me a drink and take me home for the night. I picked up my purse and not only did I leave the bar, but soon thereafter retired from the fast lifestyle. I wasn't sure what my next move would be but I didn't want to end up like that woman.

My take-away from my lived experiences as a younger woman is that claiming the crown and title "Grown Woman" is much more than simply how long one has lived, but *how* one lives, and more importantly, what she's learned on her journey and how willing she is to be honest about it.

Chapter 10

Feel the Fire - (Peabo Bryson)

David and I got through our first Thanksgiving together, our first Christmas, first New Years and first vacation. We were feeling our way and settling into a groove. I was happy not to be coming home to empty rooms, no hugs, no kisses, no one to rub my tired feet and ask, "How was your day, baby?" I was feeling brand new. I no longer kept late nights at the newspaper because I didn't have anything else to do. I loved being able to do the simple things that couples often do without having to give it a lot of thought, such as catching a movie or going for a long drive with no particular destination. It was nice not having to scrounge around for a date or having to wonder if I would receive a card or gift for Christmas, Valentine's Day or my birthday. I stopped feeling like a third wheel at parties, during which I couldn't slow dance because all the men were my friends' husbands or significant others. It was wonderful not having to wait until the deejay played the *Electric Slide*, the single ladies' national anthem, to show off my new party dress.

I was getting used to waking up and untangling myself from the pretzel positions David and I had fallen into during the night. My sleep cycle improved immensely once I learned how to regulate the rhythms of David's snoring. I would nudge him in a certain way and his breathing would shift from loud and angry to nice and easy.

"You snore, too," he insisted.

"Do not," I insisted right back. "Women don't snore."

"The hell they don't," he would say. "You snore."

Snoring became one of our running jokes. Not so funny to me, however, was David asking me to scratch his back. I hated doing it, and especially when my nails were freshly done. "Please. Please," he would beg with those hangdog eyes. He was so pitiful that I usually gave in. But when I wanted my back scratched, he did it half-heartedly and quickly feigned exhaustion.

David was something else.

He and I were getting along fine but not without differences in style and opinion. David complained about the decorative pillows on the bed. He seemed genuinely perplexed as to why I had so many pillows in different shapes and sizes. He was also puzzled as to why, if no company was expected, I insisted on making the bed up every day. It made absolutely no sense to him to make up the bed just to get back in it a few hours later.

One of David's habits that got on my last nerve was him running the washing machine for just three or four items, as if he had nothing else to wear. The machine has a setting for small laundry loads, but two pairs of socks and a pair of boxer shorts does not qualify as a small load for a washing machine. They could be washed by hand. "Hampers were created for a reason," I said. David ignored me. His way of dealing with my peeve was to wash his tiny loads when I wasn't around. I knew because sometimes he forgot to take the clothes out of the washer or the dryer. Whenever I busted him, he would look at me as if I were nuts. In that way, David reminded me of my father, whose motto for maintaining peace in the home was that a man should never confess to anything. His premise was that women may say otherwise, but they don't forget or forgive. My mother used to joke that if she caught my father on top of a woman, took a picture and shoved it in his face, Daddy would swear up and down, "It wasn't me."

Fortunately, David and I didn't have monumental differences, and so most of the time we got along. We were in love, and after so many years of no see, no hear, we had a whole lot of catching up to do and figured we had a whole lot of time to do it. That's what we thought.

Clouds were gathering just over the horizon. Six months into 2011, I understood better what my pastor, Dr. Kevin W. Cosby meant that Sunday he preached about the inescapable the cycles of life. "You're either in a storm, coming out of a storm or about to go into a storm," he said. Some people's lives are stormier than others. Sometimes their pain and wounds are self-inflicted, but more often than not, the storms of our lives arise from circumstances beyond our control, and they blow in swiftly and unexpectedly. Bad things do happen to good people.

The pages on the calendar kept turning. On April 12, 2011, I turned 65. My God, I thought, time really does fly. Some people say that 65 is "over the hill," but I celebrated my new status as a full-fledged senior citizen, an "old woman" to some, a granny to others and "Miss Betty" to young folks who were raised right. Far from being rocking-chair ready, I was rocking and rolling like a 20-year-old with David. I was in good health, still getting up and going to do work that I loved most of the time. Work that many people actually considered important and that I considered important. I was a columnist and editorial writer for *The Courier-Journal,* Kentucky's largest newspaper. My opinions were despised by some, respected by others and my life was good.

Then on June 21, the ominous clouds that had been gathering off in the far distance moved in and settled right on top of my head. I reported for work that Tuesday morning and did my usual. In my office on the first floor, I read the headlines and began pulling together ideas and materials for the column that I expected to write later that afternoon. I was about to step out for lunch with a colleague, Pam Platt, when I was summoned to the Human Resources Department.

What happened next was surreal. I was sitting in front of two people, a black man and a white woman, who were talking, but all I heard was "blah-blah-blah, blah-blah-blah," the upshot of which is that I had been kicked to the curb. When they were done with their spiel, I picked up the packet they had given me and walked around the corner to my office. I was trying to wrap my mind around what had just happened. I tried to open my computer but it had been shut down. I picked up the telephone and my extension had been disconnected. After taking some things out to my car, I tried to reenter the building, and discovered that my employee card had been deactivated. I heard that police were in the building in case one of us who had just gotten the boot got a mind to destroy equipment or worse, to shoot up the place. The added security made perfect sense.

On September 14, 1989 around 8:30 a.m., 47-year-old Joseph Thomas Wesbecker, a disgruntled and reportedly mentally deranged former pressman for Standard Gravure, a rotogravure printing company that shared the building with the newspaper, entered the plant with an arsenal of weapons, including some version of an AK47. Unable to find his bosses, the objects of his furor, Wesbecker killed eight people and injured 12 others before turning one of his weapons on himself.

Back home in New York, my mother saw news of the mass shooting, and she was a mess until I called and assured her that I was OK. By the time I arrived at the office that day, Wesbecker had already killed himself, but the building was still on lockdown.

Fortunately, in 2011 no Wesbeckers emerged from among the 700 people company-wide, including 36 in Louisville, that Gannett, *The Courier-Journal's* parent company, laid off the same day that I was. Among those laid off were journalists, advertising representatives, and other workers. Gannett was streamlining the company because daily newspapers were in free fall. Thanks to the Internet, dailies were losing readers and advertising.

I wish I had kept a journal then because much of what happened that day is a blur. David was the first person I called. "I'm on the way. Fuck them, and don't you let them see you cry," he said.

With every fiber of my being, I tried not to cry, but the elastic holding up my "big girl panties" had come undone. I didn't wail, but I did shed tears in my office. I haphazardly filled trash bags with my personal belongings, pulled books off shelves, emptied my file cabinets and tried to pack up 27 years of papers, photographs, books, magazines, awards and memorabilia.

I was in shock.

When David arrived, he stacked boxes that I had filled onto a dolly, and we rolled it out to the parking lot and put boxes in both of our cars. I wasn't able to get everything out in a single day, but a few weeks later, a former colleague was kind enough to let me into the building on a Saturday so that I could collect the rest of my stuff.

I was still numb, chagrined, humiliated, aggrieved and a whole lot of other adjectives that added up to my being one furious black woman. In the words of the comedian Robin Harris I was "pissed off to the highest of pisstivity."

As the most visible among the Louisville layoffs, because I was a high-profile columnist, my sudden exit actually made the evening news. Everyone dismissed that day was devastated, I am sure, but at least my fellow "discards" were able to grieve their lost careers outside of the spotlight. I was asked by some media outlets to make a statement. I declined.

I was angry. I was already 65 and I could have been allowed to "retire" and spared humiliation. Within days of losing my job, I also lost my life insurance and my health insurance. I received 30 weeks' severance, but the terms of my separation required me to collect unemployment and that amount would be deducted from my severance pay. I still cannot fathom how the government went along with that scam. If I happened to find another job, the severance would be withdrawn. No one offered an explanation as to why I was on the termination list, but I felt that the new leadership did not value my contribution. It was what it was.

After 30 years in daily journalism, there was no gold watch for me, no cupcakes or candles, or a mock front page filled with highlights and lowlights of my career.

In the face of what had happened to me, I recalled a joke that my friend Emma Talbott told me about an old man who had helped his congregation to build a new church. When the church opened, the man asked to make some remarks, but someone said, "Sit down, old man, nobody wants to hear from you." Stung by the rebuke and the disrespect, the old man got his hat and walked down the church's center aisle. With each step, he took his hat and hit each cheek of his behind and said, "Kiss my ass! Kiss my ass! Kiss my ass!" — all the way out the front door.

Despite my hurt over losing my job, David encouraged me to act dignified in public. "Don't give them the satisfaction of seeing you break down. You're better than that," he said.

After a few days of watching me mope around, David sat up a card table in the garage and told me to get busy sorting through the stuff I had tossed haphazardly into the boxes. He put some music on and sat with me in the garage while I ranted. He held me when I cried, recollecting all the grief I had taken from nasty readers over the years who didn't like what I had to say. Some of them had taunted me in letters and cards. They called me "nigger," "porch monkey," "fat black bitch" and other degrading names. One man harassed me for 15 years, writing letters, calling colleagues, and trying to trick me into reading what he sent by putting it in a card or using a different return address. Another reader actually contributed money in my name to right-wing organizations so that my mailbox overflowed with their racist propaganda. Who does that?

David listened when I talked about how many of us had lobbied, sometimes to the detriment of our own careers, through the National Association of Black Journalists, to keep news organizations honest in their coverage of black America and to hold their feet to the fire when it came to hiring and promoting black folks to top newsroom jobs.

Unfortunately, I told David, some of those black folks who got those top jobs turned out to be cowards in the face of white power in the newsroom. A few actually enjoyed their newfound status as newsroom HNICs, shorthand for "Head Nigger in Charge." They did little to nothing to help other African Americans get hired or advance. Matter of fact, some of them became the biggest obstacles to African American advancement in America's newsrooms. They were "handkerchief heads," shorthand for Uncle Toms, in blue suits and high heels.

David didn't know a thing about the news business, but he listened because he loved me. He let me talk myself out. He brought me colored markers to label the boxes I had brought home from the office, and then he stacked them so I could still park my car in the garage.

At the unemployment office, I ran into quite a few acquaintances and fans of my newspaper column or the local TV show that I had hosted for several years. Some offered condolences and others were incredulous. "Miss Betty, what are *you* doing here?" they asked.

I encountered so many familiar faces at the downtown unemployment office that I switched to a smaller branch closer to home. One day, the line at the small branch was snaking around the building. When I finally got inside, I could not find a seat. My back ached. My legs hurt, and I was on the verge of tears when I spied a church member staring at me. I remembered what my mother often said along the lines of the old TV commercial, "Never let them see you sweat." So, I straightened my back, and I smiled back at her.

Privately though, I was an emotional mess, and through all my messiness and crying jags, throughout that storm, David was the umbrella that kept me dry. He encouraged me to stay strong and to keep moving forward even on days when all I wanted to do was to fold into the fetal position. David was by my side every day and every night, assuring and reassuring me, in word and deed. "Don't worry, Moo, Moo. I got you."

How could I not love a man who loved me like that? In those moments, I knew that my old friend David showing back up in my life was by design.

I made history of sorts as the only member of the last fully staffed iteration of *The Courier-Journal's* editorial board who was of age but was not given the dignified option to retire. For a while, I missed the morning editorial meetings and bantering with my colleagues about everything and nothing. However, after a summer of traveling with David to visit family in Atlanta and Maryland, my healing was at hand. I had no deadlines, no nasty letters or phone calls, and I could do what I wanted to do when I wanted to do it, with whom I wanted to do it. I was getting on with my new life away from the newsroom when a few dear friends, not pleased about the way I had been separated from my career, hosted a community celebration in my honor on the campus of Simmons College of Kentucky, a private, historically black institution.

It was a classy affair. My dear friends Gail Strange, Sadiqa Reynolds, Christi Lanier Robinson and Stephanie Lackey, the organizers, wouldn't have had it any other way. Champagne flowed, and servers circulated passing out hors d'oeuvres and desserts.

My old friend Dwight Lewis, a columnist for *The Tennessean*, who had recently retired, surprised me and drove up from Nashville. I was honored with short speeches, gifts and proclamations from U.S. Rep. John Yarmuth, (D-Kentucky); Louisville Mayor Greg Fischer; Kentucky State Senator Gerald Neal, David Tandy, Louisville Metro Council President and Dr. Kevin Cosby, President of Simmons College of Kentucky. My friends and the community gave me my flowers while I was alive to smell them.

When I look through the photo album that Yolanda Demaree, my sorority sister, made for me, I see David in several pictures, standing beside or just behind me. All was well with my soul that day, and as Oprah is fond of saying, "What I knew for sure" is that God still loved me and wasn't done with me yet.

Once the shock of my separation from *The CJ* wore off and I got my finances in order, I dressed in the whole armor of God to do battle against the doubt and insecurity that comes with being fired or laid off. I felt the fire. I realized that with God, David, my family and close friends as armor-bearers, no demons from Hell could stop me from living the life intended for me. I put one foot in front of the other and strove to regain my confidence. I reassured myself that God loved me and didn't bring me that far in my life just to leave me. Being discarded from the newspaper turned out not to be the setback that I imagined, but the set-up for my next and much more important full-time job.

Chapter 11

Slow Blues - (John Coltrane)

Journalism was not the career that I dreamed of growing up. I was going to be a secretary. I was not even groomed to go to college. Now, I wouldn't trade anything for the stories that I've been able to tell or the lifelong friends I've made. I am grateful for the doors that I've walked through and the tables I've been invited to sit at, not because I was special, but because I was a member of the Fourth Estate.

I owe this writing life to the late James "Jim" Aronson, my professor at Hunter College, City University of New York. At Hunter, Jim's emphasis was on the relationship between the press and the public and the history of the Cold War. After J-School, he worked in the mainstream press, but his left-of-center political views led to him co-founding the radical weekly the *National Guardian* in 1949. I sat in Jim's classroom mesmerized by his passion for justice and his tales from the McCarthy era. He told of friends and associates whose lives and careers were wrecked when they were accused of being traitors during the second "Red Scare," the anti-communist witch hunt led by Senator Joseph McCarthy (R-Wisconsin). Jim counted among his past acquaintances the outspoken African American intellectuals W. E. B. DuBois and Paul Robeson. Jim Aronson's legacy lives on in me and in many of his former students. Most importantly, his legacy lives on through the James Aronson Awards for Social Justice Journalism that Hunter College's Department of Film & Media Studies bestows each spring. After reading the assignments I turned in for his class, Jim saw something in my writing, but I believe he liked my left-leaning politics even more. Jim took a special interest in me and added his voice to the chorus of family, friends, mentors, preachers and teachers who in various ways added new dimensions to my life. He encouraged me to pursue a master's degree at his alma mater, Columbia University's Graduate School of Journalism. Really? That was my initial thought, but then I said to myself, "Why not?" Hunter College did not have a journalism major.

I had walked past Columbia University dozens of times in the 1960s when I worked in the neighborhood. Columbia is officially located in Morningside Heights, but many also called this neighborhood "White Harlem." Not in a hundred million years did I imagine that I would attend that fabled Ivy institution. Yet, at 33 years old and 16 years out of high school, I was there in the fall of 1979 going through the rituals of my first day at the Graduate School of Journalism on 116th Street and Broadway. I didn't know a soul or quite what to expect. I had never worked in newsroom. I had not studied journalism in high school or undergraduate school. I didn't grow up yearning to be the sepia Jimmy Breslin. I had never been taught how to diagram a sentence, and the grammar I knew, I picked up as an avid reader and secretary. If my life depended on it, I couldn't explain a dangling participle. I was intimidated. I had so much to learn and not a lot of time to learn it, but I swallowed my fears and set out to be deserving of the faith that James Aronson had in me. While I learned a lot about the craft in the classroom, I learned even more in the student lounge and outside the school from my more seasoned classmates, most of whom were seven to 10 years younger. In particular, I leaned on Wayne J. Dawkins, a tall skinny kid from Brooklyn, whose love for and intensity about journalism rubbed off on me.

Black students accounted for 14.2 percent of the approximately 175 admissions into the Class of '80. The black students were close, but the class as a whole had good camaraderie. Several students, black and white, were in the habit of challenging the assertions and assumptions of such speakers as William F. Buckley Jr., the acerbic conservative pundit and founder of The *National Review*; then-New York City Mayor Ed Koch; and Roger Wilkins, the equally acerbic liberal columnist and nephew of NAACP leader Roy Wilkins.

Roger Wilkins had frequent battles with his former employer, The *New York Times.* After his visit, Dean Osborn Elliott invited someone to rebut Wilkins' assertion that *The Times* routinely discriminated against its African American news staffers. At *The Times*, Wilkins was on the editorial board and later served as editor of the Op-Ed page. He joined with other minority journalists in a lawsuit against the paper alleging racial discrimination and lack of hiring and promotion of minorities. The two sides reached a settlement, but Wilkins left the paper in 1979.

On another occasion, Dean Elliott, the former longtime *Newsweek* editor, was so frustrated by a black student's sharp questioning of a guest speaker — I don't remember which guest of the many that year — that he yelled and told the student to be quiet and sit down. That didn't go over well. I heard later that the student asked to meet with Elliott and during their conversation allegedly pointed his finger at the dean and said, "I am a black man, and don't you ever do that to me again." The alleged confrontation was all the talk for a few days.

Luther Jackson, one of the first African American journalists employed by *The Washington Post* was the J-School's first African American professor and Phyl Garland, who had forged her career largely in the black press as a reporter, editor and music critic at *The Pittsburgh Courier* and *Ebony*, was the J-School's first black female professor.

Luther and Phyl encouraged me on days when nerves and insecurities about school and other things going on in my life were distracting me from my goals. They mentored me, and my relationships with them lasted long after I had graduated. Phyl was the advisor for my master's project, which each student had to write as a requirement for graduation. She was a big sister who helped me to shape my vague ideas into my thesis about women loving men who were serving hard time.

Dear Luther encouraged me to write a book about my East Harlem life. I believe he envisioned a female version of Claude Brown's classic "Manchild in the Promised Land." This book certainly isn't that, but I believe Luther would be pleased, nevertheless, that I've taken a stab at telling some of the stories from my early life back home in Gotham.

I was about halfway through the yearlong master's program before I really began to grasp how to report and write a coherent news story. My journalistic voice was beginning to emerge.

At 33, not only was I older than many of my classmates, but many of them had at least written for their school newspapers. A few already had professional experience and were pursuing master's degrees to plump up their resumés. I was swimming upstream, and, thank goodness, more knowledgeable classmates came to my rescue. Wayne Dawkins, who had experience as a student journalist at Long Island University, commiserated with me when the legendary

Norman Issacs, my reporting and writing teacher, singled me out for criticism. One day, I turned in a story that I thought was perfectly fine. Norman thought otherwise. He read the first couple of paragraphs, glared at me, and in front of the whole class, yelled, "Bayé! What is this shit?" I was mortified and speculated that perhaps my professor was racist. Later, when I witnessed Norman publicly giving more than a few of my white classmates the blues, I concluded that my teacher was tough but fair, and I was cool with that. He did not discriminate. He was an equal-opportunity taskmaster. I passed the class.

As graduation neared, I was desperate to accumulate more news clips for my job interview portfolio than the essay about falling in love with the man who became my second husband that I had written for the 10th anniversary issue of *Essence*. Classmate Dawkins rescued me yet again. He introduced me to Andy Cooper, one of his mentors. Andy allowed me to freelance several articles for his *Trans-Urban News Service*, which provided content relevant to black Americans to the publications that subscribed to his news service.

I started J-School a couple of furlongs behind many. Thanks to caring professors and classmates who knew my handicaps, I wasn't allowed to fail. For the next the 30-plus years, I had a journalism career of which I am proud.

I found joy and passion serving the National Association of Black Journalists in various capacities, including vice president of the New York chapter; regional director; co-chair, with Sheila Brooks, a veteran TV journalist, of NABJ's first scholarship committee; president of the Louisville chapter; and ultimately national vice president for print in 1985-87.

My novel, "The Africans," was published by a major house, Dell/Banbury Books, in 1983. I co-produced and hosted "The Betty Bayé Show" on local Louisville/Southern Indiana television for several years. I won a coveted Nieman Fellowship at Harvard University and spent the 1990-91 academic year in Cambridge. I returned to Louisville after my mid-career fellowship and joined The *Courier-Journal's* editorial board, and shortly thereafter began writing a weekly column that was syndicated by the *Gannett News Service*.

I've been honored with awards for journalism and community service. Of all the accolades that I cherish, as an actor might an Oscar, or a singer a Grammy, I am especially proud to have been inducted into NABJ's Hall of Fame in 2013, and to be awarded an honorary doctor of humanities by Simmons College of Kentucky in 2016. It literally took my breath away to hear my name uttered in the same sentence as the crusading journalist Ida B. Wells.

Columbia's J-School changed my life, and the Class of '80 produced an amazing crop of reporters and writers. I still get excited when I see their bylines, their photos on book jackets, their names on rolling TV and movie credits, or learn that they've won some big award.

After graduation, a group of African American members of the J-School Class of '80 met at the West End, a bar on Broadway patronized by generations of Columbians. Over cocktails and soft drinks, we birthed the Black Alumni Network.

BAN began with a newsletter intended to keep us in touch with each other. Dawkins did the heavy lifting, publishing the monthly newsletters. By 2010, BAN members raised more than $100,000 to endow Phyllis Garland scholarships. She died in 2006. BAN was also instrumental in establishing an endowed scholarship in the name of Luther Jackson, who died in 2008.

Despite my diploma, my career in journalism didn't exactly take off like a rocket. I wasn't an eager 21-year old, and I didn't have a bunch of writing samples to show potential bosses. Some editors, based on their questions, didn't seem much interested in hiring a reporter with a background in black theater, the Civil Rights Movement and nonprofit advocacy for black folks and poor folks. One interviewer asked if I thought I could be objective covering black people, and my frustration boiled over. "No," I snapped. "Everybody knows only white people can be objective." His question was rubbish and I didn't get that job. My classmate Wayne Dawkins rescued me again. He was working at *The Daily Argus*, the newspaper of record for Mount Vernon, a suburb just north of the Bronx, and he introduced me to his editor, Nancy Q. Keefe. She liked me, appreciated my passion, but admitted that after she offered me a job, her second thought was, "What am I going to do with this woman?"

Mount Vernon, population 60,000 plus, was a fertile training ground for a cub reporter. The city's politics were rough and tumble. Parts of Mount Vernon, especially the South Side, suffered many of the ailments — poverty, drug abuse and substandard housing, to name a few — that plagued many New York City neighborhoods. I appreciated the power of the pen when stories that I wrote about a notorious South Side slumlord led to a judge sentencing him to live in one of his own buildings for a specified period of time.

Nancy Keefe took a chance on me and was a fantastic teacher. When I used "irregardless" in a story, she got right in my face and said, "There's no such word as irregardless." To this day, when I hear it spoken, or it shows up in print, I cringe. She taught me that whatever the subject of my stories — the environment, education, or politics — I should never forget their impact on ordinary people.

During my three and a half years at *The Daily Argus*, I learned to take great care writing obituaries because they are precious for the survivors and because for most people, the publication of their obituary is the only time their name will make the news.

My great joy is that my dad lived long enough to see my first bylines, and a few years later, the cover for my novel, *The Africans*.

Countless times in the decades since, I've been somewhere, for example, in the White House, or met someone, for example, like the Nobel Laureate Elie Wiesel, the Nazi hunter, and wished that I could rouse my father from his eternal slumber, and say, "Daddy, it's Boopie Girl. It's me. Guess where I am or guess who I met today?" My Dad was proud of me and told anyone willing, and even unwilling, to listen that his daughter was a newspaper reporter. Imagine that.

One of my father's acquaintances was heard to say that if I really was a reporter, why didn't he see my name atop any articles in *The New York Daily News,* the only newspaper of consequence as far as my daddy's East Harlem clique was concerned. My father eventually confronted the skeptic. The man was walking past our window, and when Daddy saw him, he called him over. Daddy reportedly said, "My daughter is so a reporter," in a voice strained and raspy from advanced lung cancer. As proof, my dad waved around copies of *The Daily Argus* that he plucked from the stack he kept in a corner in the bedroom, my mother said.

My father had long before taught me to love newspapers. His formal education ended after 7th grade, and he made up for that by becoming a voracious consumer of news and information. The radio on my father's nightstand stayed tuned to WINS 1010, which reported news and weather 24 hours a day, seven days a week, and he read newspapers every day.

New York City, when I was growing up, had several daily newspapers. The cost of *The New York Daily News* was factored into the family budget, but on his way home from work, my father would collect the other newspapers that subway riders had left behind. By the time he got to our stop, 103rd Street and Lexington Avenue, on any given day, Daddy might have tucked under his arm that day's edition of *The New York Journal-American, The New York Herald Tribune, The New York Times* or *The New York Post.*

My dad and I had a ritual for many years. We read the newspapers together, passing the various sections to one another, and then discussing current events and history. Sometimes my mother would get in on those teachable moments and tell me about the black poets and writers that she learned about in her segregated schools. Mommy was partial to Paul Laurence Dunbar, who wrote many of his poems in "Negro" dialect. She would act out and recite Dunbar's "When Malindy Sings."

My father, on the other hand, taught me about F.D.R., "The New Deal" and President Truman integrating the military. He talked a lot about World War II; Winston Churchill; Rommel, the "Desert Fox;" and Adolph Hitler. He also talked about black sports heroes. Jesse Owens, the track and field star, humiliated Hitler at the 1936 Summer Olympics in Berlin, my father said, when he outran and outjumped his white competitors to win four gold medals in track and field. Owens' feats and gold medals laid waste to Hitler's claims of Aryan superiority.

My father was a teenager glued to the radio in 1938, he said, when Joe Louis, the "Brown Bomber," knocked out the German boxer Max Schmeling in the first round of their second fight. It was as if all of Black America was in the ring. Louis' victory was another "Jesse Owens moment," as yet again, a black man on a world stage proved to be the superior athlete when the fight was fair.

Daddy revered Jackie Robinson, who desegregated Major League Baseball when he signed with the Brooklyn Dodgers in 1947. Jack Roosevelt Robinson endured the worst from outraged white fans. He persevered when some fans called him every kind of n-word and threw watermelon rinds at him, and when some players said they would rather quit than share their dugout with a colored man.

Robinson was no token. He was a star, and though privately seething from his mistreatment, he kept his dignity and excelled as an athlete. Largely because of Robinson, my father was a diehard Brooklyn Dodgers fan. When the team moved to Los Angeles in 1957, Daddy's passion for baseball waned.

I met Jackie Robinson in the early 1970s. I was chaperoning a group of youngsters from a summer enrichment program to Robinson's home in Connecticut. Mrs. Robinson, Rachael, asked a few of us if we wanted to meet her husband, who was in another part of the house. We eagerly accepted. The legend was sitting in a big easy chair wearing pajamas. Clearly in failing health, he perked up when we walked in. He didn't say much, but he flashed a weary smile and shook our hands. When I told my father about my brief encounter with Robinson, you would have thought that I had met God. Daddy wanted to know all about it.

My one-on-one conversations with my Dad were windows into his soul. He shared stories with me about his early life in Virginia, including the day that his mother, Minnie Belle Winston, died. He called his mom "Aunt Minnie" because, he said, many of his cousins lived around them and that's what they called her. Daddy said that everybody loved my grandmother's biscuits. He would get up extra early, so he could get a biscuit while it was still hot. The kitchen was separate from the house, and my grandfather, Wash Winston, had a bridge built between them so that my grandmother wouldn't have to trek through snow in the wintertime.

On this particular day, my grandmother never finished baking her biscuits. My father found her on the floor in her kitchen. He tried to wake her, but she was already gone. She had suffered a heart attack, according to the death certificate that my cousin Caroline Winston dug up while researching our family history. After her death, as was the custom back then, our grandmother lay in repose in the family home before the funeral. My father was 9 years old and traumatized.

Our mutual love of reading newspapers had made for a special Daddy/daughter bond, so I should have known that his end was near when, during the final few weeks of his life, my father didn't disturb the newspapers that I brought religiously for him to read.

Chapter 12

Everything Must Change - (Oleta Adams)

Three chairs and a desk filled the tiny office where David and I waited to learn the results of the chest X-ray and a biopsy of tissue extracted from the knot on his neck. Dr. Subin Jain, a pulmonologist, sat beside a desk in a swivel chair facing David. Their knees nearly touched as we huddled. Looking directly into David's eyes, the doctor spoke slowly, clearly and with, it seemed to me, great empathy. The biopsy revealed that David had cancer, he said. Cancer!

Whoosh! Just like that, the air seemed to have been sucked out of that already stifling little room. I put a hand on David's knee to comfort him but also to steady myself so that I wouldn't scream. I willed myself not to. As for David, he just sat there perfectly still. In the silence, I tried to read his face. He blinked a few times, but his eyes were dry. My darling was so stoic in the face of the "C-word" that I wondered if, anticipating the worst, he had medicated himself at home by smoking a joint or downing a little cognac.

David was no dummy and no stranger to unpleasant news about his health, but cancer? David knew as well as anyone that his lifestyle choices, especially decades of smoking cigarettes, left him especially vulnerable to certain forms of cancer.

David, Dr. Jain and I sat a while longer in pained silence until, all of a sudden. David stood up, shook the doctor's hand, and asked, "So, what's next?"

The events of June 20, 2013, are tattooed in my memory. That day was not the end of David's life, but the beginning of a different life, an arduous journey, for him, especially, but also for us. David would need a more-thorough examination to assess the full extent of his preliminary diagnosis. Dr. Jain obviously knew more than he was telling, but I guess he figured that he had delivered enough grim news for one day.

Dr. Jain specializes in respiratory ailments, but now David needed a different kind of doctor. He had to see a cancer specialist, an oncologist.

Just days before, David and I had returned from a busy and joyful three-week sojourn filled with sun, fun, a trip to the beach, Disney World and family reunions. Up to this point, we were having a wonderful year and were almost giddy about how our love match and our friendship had deepened. Moodles and Moo Moo were, as the kids might say, "way cool."

The year began with the annual New Year's Day open house that had become *our* open house. The people most important to me in Louisville had embraced David, and we flowed so easily together that a newcomer to our circle could have imagined that we had been a twosome for many years.

Why wouldn't the people I loved in Louisville, and who in countless ways, had shown that they loved me, welcome David into our tribe? He was a great conversationalist, when he felt like talking, and he was a good listener, precisely because he wasn't an incessant talker.

Being black and Puerto Rican made David something of an anomaly in Louisville, and perhaps to some, a man of mystery. I believe he enjoyed being a little different and a little mysterious. An old saying among bid whist players goes, "Don't let 'em peep your hole card."

My true friends seemed genuinely happy that I finally seemed to have met my match; the man that God fashioned just for me.

The opportunity for me to introduce David to an even wider circle of my friends and acquaintances had presented itself in a most wonderful way. We flew to Washington for my induction into the National Association of Black Journalists' Hall of Fame on January 17, 2013. That was one of the happiest days of my life. Besides many people from my NABJ "family," a few of my non-journalist friends also made their way to Washington to celebrate my induction. Dwight and Cora Brown, a Harlem homegirl transplanted to Louisville, flew in. Mae Jackson, my comrade from the Student Nonviolent Coordinating Committee, made it down from New York; LaVerne and Walter Vance, who had relocated from Louisville to the Baltimore area showed up, as did my cousin Caroline, Uncle Gerald's daughter, who came in from Virginia.

President Obama's second inauguration was also being held that weekend, so the District was already in a festive mood, but the Obama parties taking place that weekend didn't have anything on the red carpet that NABJ rolled out for its honorees and guests at the

Newseum, a modern, seven-story tribute to the First Amendment and the Free Press.

I had been to the Newseum several times as a speaker and mentor for the annual Al Neuharth Free Spirit and Journalism Conference for talented high school seniors interested in careers in journalism. I was always inspired by the conference theme, "Dream. Dare. Do."

Being back at the Newseum as an NABJ honoree was for me the equivalent of winning an Oscar. Thirty-three years since my entry into journalism as a newspaper reporter, I was about to be honored, along with six others, including such legends as Simeon Booker, who covered the Jim Crow South, including the torture and murder of young Emmett Till in 1955 and who was Washington Bureau chief for *Ebony* and *Jet* magazines; and the late Alice Dunnigan, the Russellville, Kentucky, native, who in the 1940s, was the first black woman reporter credentialed to cover the White House.

It was the epitome of my career to be honored by my peers. Vanessa Williams, of *The Washington Post*, my dear friend and a past NABJ president, nominated me but kept it a secret from me until the official announcement.

I loved NABJ since I attended my first convention in 1981 in, of all places, Louisville. I was new to the game and broke, but I decided that I wanted to serve the mission for which NABJ was created: to increase racial inclusion and fairness in America's newsrooms and to improve media coverage of Black America.

On that frigid night in January when I stepped forward to receive my Hall of Fame honor, David sat on the front row with a big old grin capturing the moment for posterity on his iPad. I mentioned him in my speech, recalling how he had been my rock after I lost my job. His presence that evening meant the world to me.

That was quite a weekend. Friends who hadn't attended the Hall of Fame ceremonies on Thursday and who had come to D.C. for some inaugural events stopped by my cousin Caroline's home to celebrate with me on Friday. On Saturday, DeWayne Wickham, an NABJ founder, past president and a dear friend, invited a small group of us, including David, Courtland Milloy, Vanessa Williams and my two cousins, to celebrate yet again over dinner at his home outside of Baltimore. Wickham is the founding dean of the School of Global Journalism and Communication at Morgan State University.

David and I had tickets to attend Barack Obama's on that Monday, but exhausted from all the partying, we gave our tickets to my cousin "Birdie," from Savannah, who was visiting her sister Caroline. Caroline and I had attended the first Obama inauguration together in 2009. We rode the train and then walked blocks to take our places in our assigned section. We were "way, way in the back," but we could see and hear everything on the big screens, including Aretha Franklin, wearing her gray felt hat with the big bow, singing, "My Country, 'Tis of Thee," It was freezing that day, January 20, 2009, but Caroline and I were caught up in the rapture of just being there and the very idea that a black man had been elected president of the United States. We weren't in the VIP section, but years from now, we can say that we were there in person.

On the way back to Louisville after my Hall of Fame event, we talked about some of the people we saw. David had met many of my friends, family and colleagues for the first time and made some observations. It occurred to me that David was almost as skilled as my mother in reading people, and that's saying something. When his assessments of people were less than stellar, I would try to probe him for his reasoning, but unlike my mother, David usually wouldn't say much more than he had at the outset. "I'm just offering a feeling, not a fact," he would say.

In late May 2013, David and I hit the road again. Our first stop was Atlanta, where my nephew Darnell hosted a coed baby shower to celebrate the pending arrival of his first child with his wife, Tamika Scott, an R&B singer with the group Xscape. The shower was as lavish as a wedding. David's son, Levet; daughter-in-law, Shanti; and granddaughter, Aryanna, came to the shower, and I introduced them to my sisters and cousins from out-of-town.

A few days later, David and I headed south to St. Mary's, Georgia, a quaint little town along the St. Mary's River, to visit my niece Bernadette; her husband, Kenny Cooper; and their kids, Dayvon, Destineé and Dorian, their newborn. St. Mary's boasts a cute little waterfront with a few restaurants and shops, but not much to do. We toured the area and went to the local cinema. David and I had an entire theater to ourselves watching Leonardo DiCaprio reprise Robert Redford's 1974 role as Jay Gatsby in "The Great Gatsby."

We said good-bye to the Coopers and drove south to Orlando, where a brand-new Hilton Resort would be our home for four days.

We enjoyed our suite and the other amenities, especially the resort's two swimming pools. Even so, a fevered pitchman who held us captive for two hours could not seduce us into buying a timeshare. By the time that man was done, we literally ran out of his sales office.

David had family in the Orlando area. An older sister, Josephine Mercado, a lawyer, moved with her husband, Hector, from New York to Florida in the late 1990s with the intention of retiring. "Josie" hadn't lived in the area long before she saw a need and founded a nonprofit, Hispanic Health Initiatives Inc., in 2000.

"The purpose," she said, "is to connect the medically underserved community in Central Florida with available resources." Working with a shoestring budget, Josie and her volunteers serve people who have no health insurance and no primary care providers. HHI stands in the gap by hosting health fairs, free screenings for diabetes, cholesterol, body mass index and cardiovascular disease. "We talk to them about nutrition and exercise, and we help women to get free or low-cost mammograms," Josie said.

By coincidence, or was it, two of David's nieces, Cathie Figueroa Parker, Michele Figueroa Chevera, and great niece, Ashleigh Figueroa Erickson, Michele's daughter, were in Florida while we were. It was an unexpected reunion for David with the daughters and a granddaughter of his late older brother Michael Figueroa. Michael's military service took him Fort Sill in Oklahoma. While stationed there, Michael met and married Marlene, a Comanche woman. They had seven children, including twin boys, one of whom died in infancy. David adored his big brother and on one occasion, Michael took David to spend time with his family in Oklahoma. The one thing, and it was a big thing to young David, that marred his experience in Indian country was the color-based discrimination that he said he witnessed and experienced there. Having grown up in multicultural New York, it was David's first time really feeling the sharp sting of racism. He didn't go into specifics in our conversation but clearly all those years later David was still haunted by those memories.

Cathie, an educational consultant, writes and teaches about youth violence and family wellness as those issues pertain to Native Americans. She had been invited to make a presentation to the Seminole tribe's annual conference in Hollywood, Florida. Michele and Ashleigh came along to help. After the conference, the three women came to Orlando to visit Josie and Hector and a cousin George Venitez.

"It was serendipitous," Cathie said. Indeed, it was wonderful for David. He was more jovial and talkative than usual. We visited his nieces at their hotel where we formed a prayer circle. One evening, we dined together at Disney World and took in a fireworks show afterward. Those were special days during our southern sojourn.

When I caught up with Cathie while writing this book, she told me a couple of wonderful stories about her Uncle David, such as the time she visited New York and played chess with him. "He was shocked that a high school senior beat him in five minutes." David hated to lose, especially in chess as he fancied himself an above-average player. She also recalled a Christmas vacation in Puerto Rico with her father. She recalled David and his friend Melé taking her and her sister snorkeling and to El Yunque, the only tropical rain forest in the U.S. forest system.

We didn't dare leave Florida without also visiting David's niece Karen, who lived in St. Cloud and is the daughter of his oldest sister, Catherine "Caitin" Figueroa Ruiz. Karen was at that time winning a long battle with cancer. She was very thin but energetic enough to prepare a Puerto Rican-style dinner of roast pork, rice and beans and a salad. She updated David on her health and told him she was mostly relying on natural remedies. David's cancer had not yet been diagnosed, but after he was, he and Karen talked often, swapping juicing recipes and health food recommendations. We had not intended to stay overnight in St. Cloud, but we had breakfast with Karen the next morning and hit the road.

Along the highway, I spotted a sign that said Savannah and suggested to David that we make a stop. We didn't have a set time to get back to Louisville, so why not spend a few hours in the beautiful city that had spawned the best-selling book, "Midnight in the Garden of Good and Evil?" I had visited the city in 2010 to give a speech at the 59th Annual Regional Press Institute at Savannah State University, the oldest public, historically black university in Georgia. On that occasion, I really didn't have to time to see the sights and vowed that one day I would.

The weather was fabulous. We parked the car and strolled Savannah's gentrified-for-tourists River Street. We ate ice cream and strolled through old riverfront warehouses that had been repurposed as restaurants, gift shops, art galleries and antique stores. David said that he and Diane, his girlfriend before me, regularly trolled antique stores and flea markets. I can't say that those were my favorite things to do, and I didn't let on that some of the items that elicited his "oohs" and "aahs" looked like junk to me. I had been burned enough times to know that in a relationship, it couldn't always be just about me. I'm sure David didn't always feel like doing things that I enjoyed, but he did them anyhow to make me happy.

We decided to get a hotel room, but when I called my cousin Birdie just to let her know that we were in town and planned to leave the next day, she gave us the directions to her house. She wasn't about to let us spend money on a hotel.

Birdie and her husband, Wendell DeKind, relocated to Savannah from Brooklyn in 2007. Her mom grew up in the area. My cousin brought me up to speed on the happenings on her side of the Winston family. We reminisced about our fathers and Birdie's mom, Alice aka Sister, who met my Uncle Gerald when our families all lived on Pitt Street.

I couldn't be in Savannah and not eat the regional specialty, "low-country seafood boil," a one-pot wonder of shrimp, crabs, crawfish, potatoes, corn and sausage, seasoned with Old Bay and lots of other stuff. For his part, David was craving the beach and the ocean, so Wendell, piled us into his luxury SUV the next day, and off we went to nearby Tybee Island. It was a perfect beach day. David quickly exchanged his street clothes for a bathing suit. He was one happy man when he walked into the Atlantic and huge waves greeted him. My big baby was in his element. He was deliriously happy bouncing up and down in the water.

I ventured into the water as well, but not in too deep. I know my limitations. Even so, I was far enough out for an unexpected wave to knock me off my feet. I rolled in the water like a top and kept rolling. Finally, a big wave pushed me back onto the beach. I was breathless and more than a little frightened, and everyone in our party — Birdie, Wendell, David and Birdie's granddaughter Imani — had a good laugh at my expense. I wasn't laughing, but I soon calmed down enough to enjoy the rest of the afternoon on the beach. Wendell treated all of us to dinner.

David and I made many wonderful memories during our trip to Georgia and Florida. Both of us were able to catch up with family that we didn't get to see very often.

The Tybee Island portion of our journey is memorable not just for the fun we had, but because it was there that David mentioned to me for the first time the knot on his neck. "Touch it," he said. I did and it felt hard, but since the knot wasn't huge, I wasn't alarmed. In retrospect, I probably should have been just because David brought it to my attention. He wasn't a complainer but now he was concerned enough to say that the knot was bothering him. Who knows how long that knot had been there? I thought that maybe it was a pinched nerve or the result of a bug bite. Moreover, at our ages, things just inexplicably happen. Aches and pains come and go, so one's first thought about a bump on the neck isn't likely to be, "Oh, my God, I'm dying."

I didn't have to nag David to see a doctor after we got home. He had a previously scheduled appointment with Dr. Subin Jain, his pulmonologist. His patient roster no doubt included many like David, ex-smokers who didn't quit soon enough for their lungs to overcome the damage done by smoking. After Dr. Jain examined David's neck, he suggested a biopsy for the knot and a CAT scan of his chest. Outwardly, David didn't seem to be worried about the tests, but I knew he was concerned when he asked me to go with him to get the results. When the doctor gave him the cancer diagnosis, it was the equivalent of David being run over by a tractor trailer. The sun was sitting high in the sky when we walked out of Dr. Jain's office. I suggested we get something to eat. I thought David would be hungry, but he said he wasn't. His future had quickly become cloudy and uncertain, while the sun that should have warmed us had suddenly gone cold. We were quiet on the drive home. My mother said there would be days like this, "Just keep living." I was about to climb aboard the cancer train, and I was committed to riding with David to the final stop.

My Parents 1944

"Ready for the Revolution Betty" Harlem 1969

My sisters Georgeann and Deborah flank our cousin Michelle on the monkey bars in East River

Graduation Day.
Columbia University
School of Journalism

Marrying Brian McCrary–1966

Marrying Karamoko Baye' - 1978

Channeling Nina Simone (circa early 70s)

Back home in Gotham

David's parents

5 of David's 8 Sisters at their parent's grave site in
Humacao, Puerto Rico

Young David's beautiful Afro

The Faces of David

The Faces of David

David's son called this his Dad's "campaign photo" to reel me in

Blues & Jazz Festival down by the Ohio

The King on his throne, the head of the table, after cooking dinner for four

A White Party in Atlanta

Celebrating my birthday after my knee surgery rehab

Baby let's cruise to the Bahamas (2011)

A Night Out With My Baby

My dear friend Vanessa Williams persuaded me to go my old neighborhood reunion and thus set the stage for David and I to reconnect after 50 years

Celebrating my birthday at Churchill Downs (2012)

David posing in his Steve Harvey hat

David and granddaughter Aryanna

David and Levet

David w/ Levet, daughter-in-love Shanti and granddaughter Aryanna at their home in Georgia

David Jonathan Rivera the Grandson that David didn't live to see.

David at Stone Mountain

David and I at his "Place of Peace" at Stone Mountain

"Smile baby," I said and he tried real hard. Our last photo Christmas Day 2014.

Part 2: The Journey

"Much of your pain is self-chosen. It is the bitter potion by which the physician within you heals your sick self. Therefore trust the physician, and drink his remedy in silence and tranquility: For his hand, though heavy and hard, is guided by the tender hand of the Unseen, And the cup he brings, though it burns your lips, has been fashioned of the clay which the Potter has moistened with His own sacred tears."
Kahlil Gibran, "The Prophet," 1923

Chapter 13

The Long and Winding Road - (The Beatles)

On the cancer journey, the most important relationship is that between patient and oncologist, and in my opinion, David couldn't have done better than to be in the care of Dr. Ignacio Montes. The "bromance" between the Colombian oncologist and his *Puertorriqueño* patient was evident from day one.

Before David's first meeting with Montes, we perused the thick packet of information that had come in the mail to help prepare him for what to expect. The slick brochures explained lung cancer, its causes, its stages, chemo and radiation therapies and offered nutrition and exercise tips. It also gave contact information for local and national resources available to cancer patients and their caregivers. The models depicted in the brochures were smiling, but their happy faces couldn't mask the truth that a cancer diagnosis is scary.

So, it's no wonder David was a little tense the first time he checked into Baptist Health Louisville's Cancer and Blood Disease Center (CBC). While we waited for his name to be called, I scanned the waiting room, and as the patients, old, young, short, tall, fat and painfully thin, filed in, I was reminded anew that cancer clearly does not discriminate.

David chose his oncologist based on reputation and, I suspect, because of Montes' Spanish name. When the oncologist walked into the examination room, David stood and shook his hand. It was their first face-to-face encounter, but the doctor already knew David very well from the inside out after reviewing the pathology report passed on by Dr. Jain.

Watching David and Dr. Montes interact that first time reminded me of a point that my friend, Dr. Adewale Troutman, the first African American to lead the Louisville Metro Department of Public Health and Wellness, often made. He said that patient outcomes are heavily influenced by whether the patients feel doctors care about them, listen to them and understand them. When a doctor can read a patient's verbal and non-verbal cues, the physician is demonstrating what Troutman referred to as "cultural competence." When a doctor exhibits such competence, the patient/doctor bond deepens. Such bonding, Troutman said, makes patients more fully engaged in their own care and makes it possible for the doctor to ask the right questions, make the right inferences and draw the right conclusions to tailor the treatment plan.

Dr. Montes exuded cultural competence. He was kind, compassionate and willing to answer any questions that David and I had. He and David had that *mi hermano* thing going on. They were cultural kindreds. They loved the same music, so much so that David made a CD of some Latin music for Dr. Montes. Their commonalities gave Dr. Montes the leverage to scold David about his alcohol consumption and nutrition without fear that David would be insulted and become defensive.

I smile recollecting the first time that Montes laid hands on David. He poked, prodded and after a while joked, calling David "a big boy." David laughed but his response would likely have been very different if Montes and he had no rapport. The history in America of grown men of color being called "boy" is a loaded one, and many who could not resist came to regret using that word.

Far from being anybody's "boy," David was a big man. At his first weigh in at the cancer center, David hit the scales at 317 pounds. The funny thing is that I never thought of David as overweight. He was just my big, sweet honey bear. David owed his girth to his lifelong love affair with sweets, though genetics might have been a factor, He was a diabetic who, nevertheless, answered the siren call of cupcakes and cookies, which he would eat in abundance and wash down with big glasses of 2% fat milk.

David and Dr. Montes were a great match, and David came to trust his oncologist to give it to him straight. The doctor ordered a (MRI) of David's brain and a PET scan from his "skull base to mid-thigh" These tests would provide the baseline for a treatment plan.

On David's second visit, Dr. Montes dimmed the exam room lights and used a small wand to trace the 3-D images of David's insides on a backlit monitor. The doctor said David had a mass measuring about eight centimeters, which is larger than an average-sized lime, in the "central upper left lobe" in his left lung. The PET scan revealed "bulky nodes" and "multiple additional nodes scattered through the root, the back, the middle and the front" of David's lung. "All those nodes demonstrate variable degrees of metabolic activity," Dr. Montes said.

Those findings ultimately gave a name to what was ailing my Moodles: "non-small cell lung cancer adenocarcinoma," a cancer that starts in the mucous glands inside organs like the lung, colon or breast. We learned that this form of the disease is not at all unusual for smokers and ex-smokers. According to the Centers for Disease Control, 90 percent of lung cancer deaths are in people who smoke.

We were drowning in terminology, but not so much that David and I didn't comprehend that his cancer was already far advanced. Dr. Montes put it in plain English. He told us to imagine the mass in David's lungs as the parents of the cancer that, by the time of David's diagnosis, had given birth to a bunch of mischief-making children who had moved away from home. Those cancerous "children" had settled under David's right arm, in his so-called, sub-pectoral regions, his right chest wall and his neck, which explained the "knot" that David had complained about a few weeks earlier.

The one bit of good news that day, June 28, 2013, was that David's cancer had not yet spread to his brain. Still, because his cancer had already metastasized, David knew, I knew and surely Montes knew that it would take more than man and medicine to give David a chance of living five years. David's cancer was Stage IIIB, just a tick shy of the most advanced Stage IV, when he was diagnosed.

David appeared to accept the news with resigned determination. Hysteria wouldn't change the prognosis. I attributed David's outwardly calm acceptance of his diagnosis, at least in part, to him perhaps being pleasantly surprised that he had lived long enough to collect Social Security. So many don't reach that threshold.

There it was. One minute, David and I were having the time of our lives and the next, and it did feel like just a moment, we were being peppered with big words that added up to a grave diagnosis. The mere utterance of the "C-word" has been known to reduce the strongest of men and women to tears and to temper the optimism of the sunniest personalities. We all know that we're going to die *someday,* but most of us put off thinking too seriously about that nagging fact of life. We want to have fun. We want to dance. We want to love and be loved. We want to *live.*

In my black Baptist church, we sing and shout a lot about "the sweet by and by" and what a happy day it's going to be when we meet our sweet Jesus face-to-face. Yet most of us Christians aren't in a terrible rush to die. Who wants to think about leaving the only life that we know and about leaving the people we love, the lives we've built and the materials things we've accumulated? Who wants to think about the graduations, the weddings, the baby christenings, the anniversaries and the holidays that will go on without us?

As many others were preparing for July 4th celebrations with parades, picnics and fireworks, David and I were preparing for his first round of chemotherapy.

At 8 a.m. on July 3, 2013 we were buzzed through a door at the CBC that we had never entered previously. Despite the early hour, the large, bright top floor of the cancer center was already bustling. Oncology nurses specially trained to administer the potent life-lengthening chemo concoctions flitted about. Some chatted with patients while others, after studying their orders, walked over to a room off to the side to collect the plastic bags of drugs for their patients. The bags were hung from IV poles that were attached to monitors that beeped to signal either the end of the treatment or that it was time to open the tap on a new bag.

The infusion room was lined on both sides with tiny cubicles that each contained a bed, a small table, a flat-screen TV mounted to the wall and a chair. The cubicles were for patients whose infusions were scheduled to go on for hours. David's first treatment, for example, lasted seven and a half hours. Tethered to their IV poles, most of David's fellow travelers were seated in big, comfy recliners situated within earshot and the sightline of the nurses' station in the middle of the room. Eventually, David's treatment switched to short-term infusions, and he joined those in the recliners. Over the next several months, David and I came to know the infusion room routines very well. Thankfully, the center was stocked with plenty of coffee, tea, doughnuts and other donated edibles.

David's diagnosis transformed the roles that I would play in his life. I would be caretaker, secretary, bookkeeper, driver, and with so much information coming at him, his extra set of eyes and ears. Whatever David needed me to be or to do, I wanted to be and do because I loved him. I wanted to give him fewer things to have to worry about. David's primary assignments, as I saw them, were for him to stay focused; keep his appointments, take his meds, and fight like hell for his life.

Fighting cancer is a collaborative effort. Besides Dr. Montes, the team that supported David included oncology nurses, social workers, nurse practitioners, phlebotomists, receptionists and schedulers. Not one of those professionals was superfluous to David's treatment plan. They were cheerleaders, joke-tellers, listening ears and shoulders to cry on, not just for David, but for me as well on days when the load got really heavy.

"Have a seat, Mr. Rivera," a scheduler might say, picking up the cues that David seemed a bit agitated, weary, withdrawn or overwhelmed.

"Are you comfortable, Mr. Rivera? Do you want a pillow, water, a snack?" the oncology nurses said as they prepped David for his chemotherapy infusions. One Spanish-speaking nurse on the team always greeted David saying, "*Hola!* And how are you doing today, my friend?" David would inevitably reply, "I'm good," even on days when that was a lie.

Though chemotherapy is a generalized term for cancer treatment, multiple chemo drugs are available, all with their own side effects, giving new meaning to the oft-heard observation that sometimes the cure is worse than the disease. The most obvious side effects of chemotherapy might be a bald head and the temporary loss of eyebrows and lashes, but hair loss is the least of its potentially adverse effects. Others are mouth sores, shortness of breath, joint and muscle aches, numbness and tingling of the hands and feet, severe abdominal pain, dizziness, fatigue, drowsiness, swelling of the feet and ankles, yellowing of the skin or eyes and hypersensitivity to sun rays.

David's prescribed chemo cocktail was a combination of carboplatin and Taxol, also known as Taxo/Carbo, which was to be administered every three weeks for an undetermined number of cycles.

The time had come to share with family and close friends what David was up against.

David called his son and his sisters, and tried to reach his daughter, Liza. Unfortunately, she had recently changed her phone number, so she didn't learn of her Dad's diagnosis until several days after the rest of the family. When David finally got her on the phone, I could hear Liza crying and talking very fast.

Their father-daughter conversations had never been easy from what I gathered, but I never doubted Liza's love for her father or David's love for his firstborn. Liza had already experienced the loss of her only brother, Enrique. Several years earlier, somewhere in New York, someone robbed him and beat him, and he subsequently died of his injuries. Then in 2012, Liza's mother, Sandra Roldan, died, and 18 months later, she learned that her father had been diagnosed with lung cancer. That's a lot for a child, even a grown woman with a daughter of her own to absorb.

David and I drove to New York for Sandra's funeral. David needed to be there for Liza and his granddaughter, Clachelle Alston.

Liza looks so much like David. She's tall with a "brick house" body and thick dark hair. Like David, Liza is the color of a roasted cashew nut. The scene at the cemetery was wrenching. When most of us had walked back to our cars, Liza lingered and lingered over the open grave now shared by her mother and her brother. The undertakers were noticeably fidgety, wanting to get back to the funeral home, as were the grave diggers who were standing at a respectful distance but were eager to close the hole. It was her mother, and Miss Liza Rivera would not be rushed. So, all of us waited.

David was not one to talk much about his past relationships, and as inquisitive as I am by nature and profession, I didn't press him. I pieced together, however, that Sandra and David's relationship was contentious, for reasons that were never clear to me. As children often do when their parents can't seem to get along, Liza may have felt that David had abandoned her. I can't say for sure. More than once though, I overheard David pleading over the phone, "Liza. Liza. Listen to me. Listen to me, Liza."

He was clearly frustrated about their communication failures. Even so, he was always genuinely happy when Liza called to share good news. She was getting her life together, he told me. She was going to school, getting good grades and angling to land a solid job. Liza obviously wanted her Dad's approval more than she wanted his stern lectures. "That's good, Liza, I'm proud of you," I overheard him saying during one of their phone conversations.

David's son, David Levet, also looks like David, but he's a taller and darker version. He is a realist and works in the healthcare profession on the business side. Though David was always happy to see Levet, he would chafe when his son nagged him about something. Levet knew that his father could be hardheaded, and he didn't mind telling David when he was acting stubborn. Nevertheless, when those two got together, they laughed a lot. David affectionately called Levet "Loco," Spanish for "crazy," as if that was his name, and Levet would rebut with a story about which of them was truly *loco*.

Levet recalled a day at the beach with his Dad that could have ended in disaster. David got so distracted joshing with his friends that he failed to notice little Levet floating away from the beach wearing the inflatable life jacket that David had "liberated" from an airplane. (Who does that?) Finally, someone spotted the crying boy, and yelled, "Hey, man, is that your son?" David swam out and rescued Levet from the water, and then begged the boy not to tell his mother, Juanita Cruz-Cataquet. She would have killed him, Levet said.

David's younger sisters — Crimilda "Cookie" Rivera Torres, Maria Irene Rivera, Benigna "Beni" Rivera Zeno and Milagros "Millie" Rivera — were devastated when David told them that he had cancer. Those women worshipped their big brother. They had grown up with him in the household after their older siblings had married and moved out. David was their entertainer, their candy man and their protector because their father, "Big David," was often away at sea.

David also announced his diagnosis to his older sisters, Caitin, Josie and Lydia. All the sisters worked hard to keep his spirits up. Whenever David's younger sisters; daughter Liza; and David's niece Lydia Maria Franklin, Cookie's daughter, known as Giga, called, often on FaceTime, they tried to give him something to smile about. They told stories about David bringing them sweets, messing with their dolls, tucking the girls in bed and singing to them.

Millie reminded David of the time when she was 8 or 9 and was about to drop kick a boy who had been harassing her all year at school. David walked up on the altercation and intervened. He scooped little Millie up in his arms and carried her, kicking and screaming, upstairs to their apartment.

"I was so mad," she said. "I was mad at the boy, and I was mad at my brother. I just wanted to get that kid." That story brought a smile to David's face and tears to his eyes.

David left it to me to tell my sisters about his condition. They loved their "brother-in-law." Like me, Debbie and Georgeann had known David since they were little girls running around the projects. What they did not know until David and I reconnected is that I also knew David and that I had crush on him when we were kids.

My sisters and I were no strangers to lung cancer. Both our parents, who chain-smoked unfiltered Pall Malls in the red pack, succumbed to the disease. Everyone's cancer journey is different, but when our father battled the disease in the early 1980s his treatment was primitive, compared to my mother's in the mid-1990s, and even more so to David's in the 21st century.

No one has found a cure for cancer, but even from my lay perspective, I can see that progress is being made.

After two cycles of chemo, David underwent yet another CT scan. He was given a prescription to treat nausea from the chemotherapy and was instructed to buy over-the-counter drugs to combat constipation, fever, pain and diarrhea.

Every cancer patient's chemo plan has goals. For some, it is to try to remove all traces of cancer, and for some others the goal is to "suppress the development of secondary cancerous tumors." The goal of David's chemo plan was "palliative." In other words, his treatments were intended to provide him some measure of relief "from the symptoms and stresses" as his cancer progressed.

I kept track of David's medical paperwork in a folder, but I never saw his chemo plan until more than a year after he died. I was reviewing some of the papers related to his medical procedures. It was dated June 27, 2013. I'm not sure how that piece of vital information was kept from me. Was it purposeful? Sitting there reading the plan, I realized that from early on in his journey, David knew that, absent a miracle, and miracles have been known to happen, long-term survival was not an option.

Did David fear that I wouldn't be in it for the long haul if I knew how grim his prognosis was? Did he fear that I would leave him?

Chapter 14

You're All I Need to Get By - (Marvin Gaye & Tammi Terrell)

For the rest of 2013, David and I paddled upstream into unfamiliar and troubled waters. I was shuttling him to his various medical appointments, including 40 hours of chemotherapy between July 3 and December 12.

Through it all, David was stoic. His tolerance for pain astonished me. "It is what it is Moo Moo," he said apparently hoping to ease my fears. He calmed his own emotional waters by retreating into his man cave for hours, playing chess on his computer or listening to praise songs out of Africa and the Caribbean.

I had more confidence in David's ability to navigate his cancer than I did in mine to handle the lurking fear of what would come next. When I left David to go shopping or to a meeting, I feared what I might find when I got home. I secretly looked for changes in his physical appearance. Inquiring eyes wanted to know. Sometimes I hugged him tight, and asked, "How you feeling, Moodles?" The question annoyed him and probably came off as me nagging but trying to be cool about it. His answer was always the same. "I'm good," he would say and then flee into his cave and turn his music up a little louder.

We both needed the spiritual energy of music, all kinds of music, to keep some semblance of balance as David stared down his Goliath. The Puerto Rican singer La India's salsa version of Charlie Chaplin's "Smile" was cued up on David's playlist almost every day. We were keeping a pretty grueling pace and found solace in the lyrics.

David despised my old-fashioned and extremely loud alarm clock, but its wake-up squeals were indispensable to the new rhythms of our lives. With so many appointments to keep, David and I pretty much stuck close to home and terribly missed our little getaways. But we made a point not to be antisocial. When we felt up to it, we made the local rounds. His efforts to keep up his spirits and mine were Oscar-worthy.

In addition to his chemo drugs, David took plenty of other medicine. I can't say that he took them all at the same time, but his list included nine different medications. David also took such "natural healers" as milk thistle to lower his cholesterol, fish oil to lessen his chances of suffering a stroke and turmeric root extract for his arthritis, joint pain and fatigue. Marijuana and brandy were not on his official medicine list, but David self-prescribed them.

Shortly after my induction into the National Association of Black Journalists' Hall of Fame, I received an over-sized basket of spirits from Remy Martin. The card that accompanied the beautifully packaged bottles of cognac congratulated me on my honor. As a lifelong teetotaler, I decided to save the cognac for guests on very special occasions. When such an occasion arose later that year, I discovered that David had been treating himself to the cognac. Every bottle in the basket was empty. David hid his duplicity by putting the empties back into their original containers. When I confronted him, all he offered was one of his "Who me?" expressions as if someone else, a ghost perhaps, had drunk all the cognac. I wanted to wring David's neck, but the silly expression on his face dissipated my anger. He was like a kid who swears up and down that he didn't drink the last of the cherry Kool-Aid, even though his tongue and lips are red. Given all the medicine that he was taking, all the reefer he was smoking, and all the liquor he was drinking when I wasn't around, it's a wonder that David wasn't glowing in the dark.

Through it all, my sweetie got up every day, put one foot in front of the other and kept moving as best he could. David's cancer was an ever-present reality, but it was not all-consuming. On his best days, we would go out to dinner and to the movies, where no sooner were the lights dimmed than David would fall asleep and snore. When the snoring got too loud, I tapped him on his arm or thigh, and he would wake up and pretend that he was just "resting his eyes" and knew what was happening on the big screen. We went to birthday and retirement parties, weddings, a couple of concerts and University of Louisville men's and women's basketball games. Most people who saw us out had no idea about all the demons that David was fighting at once. He put up a good front. He wasn't fighting one Goliath, but many that had the potential to take him down. Only he and I knew what it really took for David to get dressed, go out and smile.

Cancer met a formidable foe in David Rivera. He had never been a whiner or a punk, and he wasn't going to go down easy. He was a street fighter down to the bone. I loved that about him, even at times when he had plucked my last nerve. David's general demeanor exuded a toughness that helped to strengthen me for the journey. I felt safe with David even as his illness progressed. All men definitely *are not* created equal.

David never talked much about his cancer directly, other than to say that he never wanted to be a burden. I always tried to reassure him, even when, to be honest, I was really tired, really scared and really overwhelmed. I thought of myself as his lieutenant, his second in command. David was what young people refer to as an "old player." He was not in the habit of ordering up violin music to accompany his sad stories.

"Everybody's got a life, and everybody's got a story, but I'm still here," he would say.

David kept soldiering on without blaming everyone else for his conditions when he knew good and well that much of what ailed him was the result of his poor choices. Some people get a toothache and complain so much that you want to shoot them.

David's resilience most of the time was matched by my mess of emotions. I would be brave one day and scared half to death the next. I careened between great hopefulness and great despair. In my hopeful moments, I could almost convince myself that David would defeat the cancerous army that had set up outposts in the upper regions of his body. I could imagine David having a lot more time to live, laugh and love with me. We were good people. We weren't perfect, but we hadn't killed anyone. Hadn't I heard of and read about people with cancer who managed to beat it and live productively for years and even decades? So yes, hopeful Betty asked, "Why not David?"

My consolation was also knowing that plenty of people never experienced the love that David and I shared during the time we had. As tough as it was many days on the journey, David managed to hand me sweet surprises. One awaited when I returned from Delta Sigma Theta Sorority's 100th anniversary convention in Washington, D.C., where the sorority was founded in 1913 by 22 African American women at Howard University. As one newspaper article said, the District was awash in our colors, crimson and cream. While I was away, David and Levet, who had come up from Atlanta to hang out with his Dad, planted perennials in the little flower garden in back of the condo. I don't know a thing about flowers, but it had yellow, white, red, purple and orange ones.

"Do you like it?" David asked, stepping aside to let me soak in their masterpiece. I suspect that David's contribution was mostly supervising and that Levet did most of the planting.

"Oh, baby. I love it. It's beautiful," I said, meaning every word. Indeed, it was a sweet, sweet homecoming.

After David had fallen off to sleep, Levet shared with me that those few days alone with his Dad had been cathartic. They had done some soul-to-soul talking and gone all the way back into the dusty vault of their lives together and apart. They apparently were able to clear up some issues that had vexed Levet for years. Though not all of David's explanations as to why he did or said certain things fully satisfied Levet's quest for clarity, their time together was precious if not perfect.

David and I enjoyed that little flower garden. It's a gift that keeps on giving, though I must admit that it's never been quite as beautiful as it was the first time it was planted. It was a conscious choice not to have a TV on the patio/porch. I planned that space for morning coffee, conversation, contemplation, meditation and listening to music.

When I set up the porch, I had my mother's sister, Aunt Loretta, in mind. On one of my visits to Maryland, my aunt brewed a pot of coffee and invited me to sit with her on her tiny enclosed back porch and I fell in love with the idea. We talked quite a while that morning as we sipped coffee out of tea cups from my aunt's fine china cabinet. Aunt Loretta had a fondness for nice things — Cadillacs, mink coats, diamonds, meticulously manicured nails, silk pajamas and pretty lounging robes. She wouldn't be caught dead in some flowery housecoat. To see her in her middle years, you would never believe that when she was growing up, her nickname was Dukie because she often "put up her dukes" to fight.

We even called her Aunt "Dukie." My mother said that one day my aunt was acting up in school, and the teacher ordered her to sit in the coat closet until the school dismissal bell rang.

"Do you know that my sister sat in that closet and patiently cut the fur off the teacher's coat with a pair of children's scissors. Papa was mad. He had to pay to get the teacher's coat repaired," mom said.

Aunt Loretta's response to stories about her fighting days was to say, "I don't remember," and my mother would accuse her of suffering from "selective amnesia."

It didn't occur to me back then that those were the halcyon days of my life and that it wouldn't be very long before all my aunts and uncles would be gone and I would never, at least on this side of Glory, get to sit, listen and learn, or have them love on me again.

When the summer of 2013 turned to fall, visitors came from the East, and David was overjoyed to welcome to Louisville his nephew Erin (his sister Irene's son); Erin's wife, Jackie; and their baby boy, Amari. The family was headed to Texas for one of Erin's U.S. Air Force assignments. David had attended the young couple's wedding in New York two years earlier. I didn't go with him but was able to enjoy the festivities on television. The big event and the preparations leading up to it were filmed as a Spanish-language reality series.

In preparation for the first visit by members of his family, David shopped at Mi Preferida, a nearby market that specializes in Latin foods, drinks and spices for the meat and ingredients he needed to prepare a traditional Puerto Rican dinner.

The housed reeked of garlic, onions, oregano and adobo seasoning. When he was done cooking, we sat down, in the dining room, of course, to a hearty meal of slow roasted *pernil* (roast pork shoulder), beans, rice and fried plantains. David sat at the head of the table. He was the king of the castle and he loved his position.

There's something about having a baby in the house that brings life and laughter to the inhabitants. I took a photo of David holding Amari on his lap, and they bore a striking familial resemblance with their smooth faces and wrinkly foreheads.

David was feeling well enough the next day to ride along when I gave Erin and Jackie a brief tour of the city. I showed them Churchill Downs, the Ohio River waterfront and Old Louisville, a section of the city with the stately homes of St. James Court with its signature wrought-iron fountain, as well as the nearby University of Louisville's

Belknap campus. The oval in front of U of L's administration building is dominated by a 6-foot, 7-inch tall bronze cast of the French sculptor Auguste Rodin's "The Thinker" resting on a pedestal of almost equal height. The next day, Erin, Jackie and Amari set off on the next leg of their long drive west. No doubt, they could see how much their visit had done to lift David's spirit.

We were sorry to see Erin and his family leave, but it wasn't long before others who loved us came to visit. My cousin Gloria Pinder Jackson, a longtime cancer survivor, flew in from Atlanta to spend a few days. In November, my dear friend Vanessa Williams, flew in from D.C. — not the former Miss America, but the journalist, and the one that I refer to as the *real* Vanessa Williams, the deep chocolate one. To David's sheer delight, Vanessa brought her dog/daughter CeCe. She's a Havanese that V named in honor of the fabulous Cuban-born singer Celia Cruz.

David loved dogs and desperately tried to talk me into getting one. Each time he asked, my answer was an emphatic "No!" Call me selfish, but I live by the motto, "To thine own self be true."

I didn't grow up with a dog, and I'm afraid of dogs in general except for Vanessa's CeCe. Plus, I fully expected that I would end up being the dog's primary caretaker. I pictured myself in sleet, snow, ice and rain having to walk the sweet little beast and then having to wait around holding a plastic sack and disposal rubber gloves to pick up dog poo. No way did I want responsibility for a dog. For the record, I also don't want goldfish, gerbils, turtles, cats or indoor plants, which I have been known to murder either from over-watering or forgetting to water at all.

Though I love my *forever* First Lady, Michelle Obama, I do not have a green thumb and I am not "Becoming" an urban farmer. I'll continue buying my fruits and vegetables from Sam's Club or Kroger's, thank you very much.

Shortly after Vanessa and CeCe flew back east, Ronald and Pat Richardson stopped by on their way from Chicago to North Carolina. Ron's family and mine lived in the same building in the projects in East Harlem. Ron's career in banking took him to Chicagoland years ago.

When company came, life felt normal. If David was feeling poorly at those times, he kept it to himself. Thoughts of cancer, chemotherapy and all things related to David's fragile health receded into the background when he played "the host with the most." Breaking bread, listening to music and swapping our "remember him, remember her, remember this, remember that time that we did such-and-such?" stories were antidotes for what ailed us. I loved it when David laughed so hard that his belly shook, and tears ran down his cheeks.

With friends and family around, we exhaled, and David, at least for a while, was "old" David, singing in the kitchen, offering toasts and pontificating about anything and everything.

By mid-December, David had completed his scheduled chemotherapy regime.

"Thank you, Jesus!'

He did it. He looked fairly good and strong. With that behind him, the big "red light" turned green, allowing us to get out of town for Christmas.

The change of scenery did us good. We stocked the car's CD player with Christmas music by the Temptations, the Whispers, Natalie Cole, Pattie LaBelle and Kem, and we hit the road to Georgia to visit David's son.

We would know soon enough if those 40 hours of chemotherapy had the intended effect of killing off the cancer or at the very least slowing it down.

David was a very happy traveler. He didn't have to drive, so he laid back and chilled. He also flirted with "the chauffeur" and had the audacity to complain about the funky state of my car. He always complained about the candy wrappers and the residue of chips and pretzels that had lodged between the seats and the console.

"That's why the animal chewed up the steering wheel," David reminded me, re-opening a sore spot. It was true that a critter of some sort had gotten into my car, perhaps through the tailpipe, and wreaked havoc. Whatever that animal was, the thing chewed on the leather steering wheel and upholstery. Fearful that the creature might still be in the car, I stood in the garage and commenced to screaming, "David! David!"

My hero came running in his underwear wielding his big switchblade and the Louisville Slugger bat that he kept on his side of the bed. It was freezing outside, and David reasoned that the poor critter was just looking for a warm spot and was seduced by the particles of junk food that I was in the habit of eating and drinking while driving. The last thing I needed in the moment was David being rational.

I had owned several cars, but none had ever been attacked by an animal. I argued against David's logic, but only a little, because in my heart I knew that he was probably right. Even so, I was terrified by the thought of what could have happened if the animal had jumped out while I was driving. Just in case the whatever was still hiding out under the seat, in the trunk or in the tailpipe, I sprinkled poison pellets around the car that I hoped the creature would munch on and die. The critter, whatever it was, never showed up for an encore.

Meanwhile on our road trip, whenever we stopped for gas, coffee or food, David would slip off. Did he not know that I could smell reefer? Sure, he did, but David was a very sneaky dude, and not just with his reefer smoking. He also hid from me how much he was gambling on the lottery. It was his money, and God knows the cause was good. In Kentucky, the money goes to public education. Funding for public education in the state is very inadequate. Kentucky is always near the bottom among the states for educational attainment.

David did win every now and again. He shared a couple of nice-sized payoffs with me. However, after David died, I found wads of losing lottery tickets stashed throughout the condo. Finding those tickets reminded me of Richard Pryor's joke about what his dog did when the comedian was breaking up with one of his several wives. Before leaving with the wife, the dog went off to a corner and did its business. Pryor said that on its way out the door, the dog looked at him and said something to the effect of, "Hey, Rich, I thought I'd leave a little something for you to remember me by. You were always tardy with the food." Well, David left a lot of losing lottery tickets for me to remember him by.

The best thing about our Christmas trip to Georgia is that David seemed well the whole time. I took plenty of pictures, but my favorite is of David and his son standing shoulder to shoulder in Levet's living room. Stenciled on the wall just above David's left shoulder is the word LOVE and beneath that, in smaller letters, the word "Faith." It wasn't an intentional backdrop, but God knew that David and I would need not just any kind of love but profound love and faith in abundance during the months to come. We left Georgia in time to be home for New Year's.

Chapter 15

Joy and Pain - (Frankie Beverly and Maze)

When daylight broke that first day of 2014, I was feeling sort of normal. David had completed six months of rigorous chemotherapy, and he was still on his feet and still making me happy most of the time. He was asleep and breathing easy for a change. I looked over and thanked God for reconnecting us. He was the missing piece of the jigsaw puzzle of my life that I didn't even know was missing until David showed up again out of the blue. It was a new year, and David and I were grown folks loving as grown folks are freed up to do. We were pressing on. We didn't sit up every night fretting about what others thought about our relationship. David was the love that I had been waiting for.

On that New Year's morning I contemplated the busy day ahead trying to get everything in order for our open house. I still had much to do. I took care not to wake David too early. I used that small window of quiet time to pray for a successful gathering and to consider once more just how much the man on the other side of my bed had come to mean to me.

Life with David before and after his cancer diagnosis had given me not just new, but profound insights into the who and why of my very existence. After many years of living alone and doing whatever I wanted to do, through my relationship with David, I realized my capacity to share and endure.

Until David came back into my life, for example, it had never occurred to me that for most of my adult years I had been a stingy lover. That is to say, that while I felt deeply for some of my male companions, and perhaps imagined that I had loved a few, I had never really given 100 percent of myself to any man. I realized that I was never as trusting as I had always imagined myself to be. I was never *all in* for those relationships. If I had been, I cannot imagine that it would have been as easy to walk away and, quite often, never to look back. If I had been *all in*, it should have been harder and hurt more to say good-bye, farewell, so long, adios, see you later alligator, to the men in my life.

If I was giving 100 percent of myself to my lovers, I should have needed more time to recover when those relationships died or just faded away. I won't claim never to have experienced heartbreak; I did. Nevertheless, none of my break ups, not even from my two husbands, broke me. I never felt suicidal or told myself that I never wanted to try love again.

When David came, I finally laid all my cards on the table. For whatever reason, age perhaps, I wasn't afraid. David's black magic, I guess, is that I knew him when, and he knew me when, so I felt safe with him. Is that too much to ask? Surely, other women crave that sense of safety with a man as much as we crave love itself. David was not mean, competitive or emotionally abusive.

Even when he wasn't being intentional, David was always teaching me something. He didn't pretend to be what he wasn't. Most of all, David was my friend. He was my protector, my Jack Johnson and Muhammad Ali rolled into one. He was my big, handsome fighter from back on the block who retreated to his corner every now and then to lick his wounds and await the bell that signaled the next round of the fight of our lives. for his life.

I looked forward to a new year with my sweetheart. Whatever 2014 portended, we were David and Betty, Moodles and Moo Moo, a team, and we would weather our circumstances together.

By the time the first guests for our New Year's Day open house arrived, David and I were ready, but well before the last guests bid good night, David was down for the count and snoring. It had been a long day. I turned the lights out and climbed into bed, achy, but happy. I crept into the crook of David's arm, and he budged just enough to adjust and make space for me in my safe place. The steady rhythm of his snores eventually lulled me to sleep.

Our sweet respite was short-lived, however. Two days after New Year's, we were back at the cancer center for the read out of the CT scans that had been taken of David's chest, abdomen and pelvis in late December. For the rest of January and into February, we made more visits with the oncologists, and David had lab tests, medicine reviews and a few more hours of chemotherapy.

If I was wearing down emotionally from all the back-and-forth and the tense moments awaiting the results of one test or the other, David surely had to be exhausted. Yet the two of us would sit in that, by then all-too-familiar, waiting room, watching TV, drinking the free hot chocolate or coffee and making small talk. We were in combat mode, and I was still praying for a miracle. No doubt the others that we encountered in the cancer center waiting room were keeping God busy praying for miracles, too.

More than a few of David's fellow travelers looked to be in far worse shape than he was. Some were as pale as onion skin and some seemed so fragile that a gentle wind would blow them off their feet. My Moodles, on the outside at least, was still looking fairly robust. He had lost some weight since his diagnosis, but David was still a big dude.

One morning at the cancer center, we ran into a former newspaper colleague of mine. I was so happy to see him and assumed that he had escorted a family member or perhaps a friend to the center. Surely, Joe Ward didn't have cancer. He was the guy at the newspaper who put the rest of us to shame by bicycling to work almost every day. He had the lean physique that suggested healthy eating and, if he drank at all, I just imagined it was in moderation.

Simply put, my former colleague was the polar opposite of David, and yet there he was at the CBC fighting for his life too. Cancer etiquette dictated that I not ask Joe what type of cancer he had, and he didn't volunteer to say. I introduced Joe and David. A few weeks later, Joe was dead. It broke my heart because he was one of the good guys. I never shared the news of Joe's passing with David, but I attended Joe's memorial service at one of Louisville's historic mansions. The event was a mini-reunion of former and still-employed *Courier-Journal* staffers.

By late February, David's cancer journey entered a new phase. We were directed into a windowless conference room on the first floor of the cancer center. We weren't quite sure what to expect when Dr. Ben Birkhead, a radiation oncologist, sat down at the opposite end of a conference table to tell us David's cancer had spread to his brain and to discuss what would come next. A new team of caregivers would work in concert with Dr. Montes and the oncology team on the top floor.

After reviewing David's records, Birkhead's treatment plan called for 13 rounds of radiation to David's brain. The new team would include a medical oncologist who would manage David's radiation care and a radiation oncology nurse who would conduct

David's check-ups and instruct him about what to expect from radiation therapy, including the potential side effects and how to manage them.

It was a lot to absorb for one day. We were scheduled to come back the next day, giving David overnight to think about whether he wanted to go forward with radiation. Many people opt not to. My mother was one. My father, back in the 1980s, was burnt almost to a crisp by radiation to treat his lung cancer. After seeing that, Mom in the mid-1990s, wanted no parts of radiation to treat her lung cancer, even if it might have permitted her to live a little longer.

David's doctors mapped out the strategy for his treatments. The skin on his neck would be tattooed with permanent ink, and a customized mask made for him to wear during treatments to limit damage to other tissues near where radiation would be applied. These preventative measures definitely were an upgrade from my father's practically stone-aged radiation regimen.

I had a general idea of what was going to happen after David kissed me and disappeared down a hallway that I wasn't permitted to walk with him. David never told me in any specificity what took place during his radiation treatments, but I did my own research and watched videos of the process for patients like David with cancerous tumors in their necks or heads. The mesh radiation masks are carefully marked to assure consistency from one treatment to the next. The masks resemble, at least to me, the thick, wide-holed hairnets that many women back in the day tied around their heads to keep their roller sets in place. Though the process is reportedly painless, patients must lie still inside the machine that delivers the radiation during the treatments, which average 15 minutes. So, the masks are affixed to the table to hold patients' heads in place to ensure that the radiation beams are accurately directed to the specific area or areas mapped out in the patients' treatment plans.

If David was ever anxious during his radiation treatments, he never mentioned it to me. That was so like him. I'm sure he figured that the less I knew, the less I would have to worry and nag him about.

While the list of the potential side effects of radiation therapy is long — everything from dry mouth, trouble swallowing to ear pain — David experienced few things on the list. He did suffer with dry skin, and he loved for me to massage and moisturize it. He also had occasional hoarseness and fatigue. Because he was already mostly bald before being diagnosed with cancer, his additional hair loss was barely noticeable. In fact, I thought that David looked more handsome with a smooth face and a thinned-out mustache.

While his treatments continued, my left knee was causing me pain, but I had put off replacement surgery. My hesitation was that David was under doctors' orders not to drive because of the effects of radiation therapy, as well as his medications. Not only would he risk harming himself, but in the unfortunate event of an accident, he would be criminally liable. I knew David would be tempted to get behind the wheel, because he had an ornery streak and because I'm not sure that he ever fully comprehended how sick he was. For the most part, he didn't look sick because the chemo and radiation therapies didn't knock him out.

The time came, however, when I had to make my knee surgery the priority. All I could do was pray that David would be safe while I recovered. How would David get around while I was in the hospital and then in rehab for 10 days? We got him set up for Louisville Metro's door-to-door bus service for seniors. I still feared that David would drive himself for the quick trips.

As God would have it, the cavalry arrived in the persons of David's baby sister, Milagros, "Millie," and her life partner, Kathy. They drove in from New York.

Millie knew her big brother well. She and Kathy came bearing sweets for David and for me. They bought chocolate jelly rings for David and a Junior's Famous Cheesecake for me. My sweet-a-holic devoured his treat in no time flat, Millie said and desperately wanted to get at my cheesecake. Millie wouldn't let him have it, and the cheesecake survived so that when I came home from rehab, we stuck a candle in it, and it became my birthday cake as I turned 68.

After Millie and Kathy left, David and I stayed close to home throughout that spring and summer. He kept his appointments for routine check-ups at the cancer center, but he had no more chemo or radiation treatments. By no means was he healed, but the treatments had kept the cancerous invaders at bay.

I was hoping to get out socially a little more. Every first weekend in October, thousands of people converge on the historic and gracious Old Louisville neighborhood for the St. James Court Art Show. Creatives of every stripe, from fine artists to furniture makers, vie for precious spots to display and sell their eclectic offerings. Dating to the late 1950s, the St. James art show has evolved into a really big deal. More than 700 artists from across the country are featured and potential buyers come in search of clothing, jewelry or works of art that quite often are one of a kind. The St. James art show is the portal to fall in Louisville and a perfect excuse to don a new sweater, carve pumpkins, sip hot cider and down heaping bowls of homemade chili and potato soup.

In 2014, Dr. Adewale and Denise Troutman came back to town for the art show. The Troutmans relocated to Tampa when he was appointed director of the University of South Florida's Public Health Practice and Public Health Leadership Institute. Ade and Denise had been a power couple in Louisville. He was director of the Metro Department of Public Health, the first African American to head the department, and she was president and CEO of the Center for Women and Families, which serves victims of domestic violence. In Louisville, I interacted with the Troutmans professionally and socially through a network of mutual friends. I felt a special kinship with Doc because he's my homie. I don't recall meeting him in New York, but we traveled in the same circles during the political and cultural renaissance in Harlem in the late 1960s and 1970s. When the National Black Theater, of which I was a member, performed at the world-famous Apollo Theater on a bill headlined by Little Richard, Ade said that he was one of the drummers who played for NBT's performance.

When I heard that Ade and Denise were in town for the art show, I was excited at the opportunity to break bread with them at a dinner party in their honor hosted by Nat and Chandra Irvin. The Irvins had become a power couple in their own right since arriving in Louisville from North Carolina.

Nat is many things, notably a composer and beloved professor in the University of Louisville's School of Business. His specialty is studying the future and making predictions based on current trends. He is the only African American "futurist" that I know. Chandra, meanwhile, is a consultant who teaches strategies for uniting people from diverse backgrounds and beliefs. She exudes spirituality. I am always eager to be in the company of brilliant and kind people, but when I got the invitation, I wasn't sure David was up to it. I told him I really wanted to go, and he readily agreed to be my date. David had been battling cancer for more than a year, and it had been a while since we had stepped out together socially.

Perhaps it was the lighting or maybe it was that the Irvins' house is more spacious than our condo, but that evening I really noticed how much David's appearance had changed. I saw him every day and seemed to have missed that his complexion had become sallow, that his eyes had lost their brightness, and that his gait was slow and uncertain. His thin sweater hung loosely against his frame. How did I miss what was right before my eyes? I had failed to notice his fragility, and he had taken great pains to hide it from me. In retrospect, I was most certainly in denial.

David didn't do much talking over dinner, but he was engaged. "You OK, baby?" I whispered.

"I'm good," he said, annoyed that I had asked him the same question two or three times during the evening.

Even so, I kept an eye on David, not wanting to miss a silent cue that he was tired and ready to leave. It was a lovely dinner, somewhat muted by my concern about David's physical decline, as well as the jaw-dropping news that Doc Troutman had recently been diagnosed with Parkinson's. Say Parkinson's to most Louisvillians and images of the GOAT (The Greatest of All Time) immediately spring to mind. Muhammad Ali, born and reared in Louisville, symbolized to the whole world the ravages of Parkinson's, but he also evidenced how long certain people manage to outrun the disease that wreaks havoc on the nervous system. Ali was diagnosed in 1984 and lived another 32 years. My prayer for Doc is that he will live to be 100 and have the last laugh.

Denise and I warmly embraced. We needed no words to remind us that our men, our big, strapping, handsome, strong men, were forever changed and that our lives with them would be very different up ahead, and perhaps at times, excruciatingly painful. That reality was nearer than I imagined.

Chapter 16

Angel of Love - (Michele Columbier featuring Phil Perry)

About a week after Nat and Chandra's dinner party, David fell at home. It wasn't the first time he had fallen, but this fall was horrific. It was early morning, and I was still half asleep. Startled, I jumped up and ran to the other side of the bed. Oh, my God! David was on the floor. His head had barely missed the nightstand, but he had smashed his trash can into a virtual piece of modern art fashioned of black metal and mesh. David had lost some weight, but he was still a big guy, and the two of us working in tandem couldn't get him off the floor. He was breathing heavy and the initial look of helplessness on his face quickly dissolved into sheer terror as he kept struggling to hoist himself off the floor. He pulled at the comforter and the sheets to no avail.

He had been on his way to the bathroom and had taken only a few steps when he went down *hard,* so hard, in fact that the room shook. It didn't help matters that now the floor was slippery because, unable to get to the bathroom to urinate, he was lying in a puddle trying to catch his breath and hopefully gather sufficient strength to try again to get up. Together, we tugged, and we pulled, but we just weren't strong enough. Finally, he looked up at me and held his arms out as if to say, *"No mas"* (no more).

I wasn't able to help David in that terrible moment. All I could do was cry. We were exhausted from our efforts and finally had to surrender to the truth. It was a hard surrender. I dialed 911. David wasn't happy about that. His Puerto Rican *machismo* reared up. He didn't want to go to the hospital, but I turned deaf ears to his protests.

A previous fall in the bedroom happened when David tripped on a rug. On that occasion, I called Rod Strickland, my friend and personal trainer, who lived nearby. Rod was a listening ear for my updates about David. He had visited David on occasion and a few times helped David to get his car running. Rod was busy with a client, but asked his wife, Angie, a licensed nurse practitioner, to come to the house. Angie and their son, DeVonte' arrived fairly quickly. Angie checked David's vitals, and though he was obviously shaken up from falling, she didn't think David merited a trip to the hospital.

There was another scare the day that I returned from a quick trip to the grocery store and found David half on and half off the bed, frothing at the mouth and convulsing. His eyes were rolling around in his head and he couldn't speak.

I called 911 and within minutes two emergency medical technicians were rushing in. One shined a light into David's eyes. "Is he a diabetic?" he asked. "Yes," I said and added that David had lung cancer. The medic concluded that David was having a low blood sugar episode that may have been brought on by all the different medications he was taking. The medic went into his bag and gave David something to bring his sugar level up. David responded quickly. The EMTs stayed a little longer to make sure that David was stable. As the medics were leaving, I told them that David acted a little weird before I went to the store. I asked David something, and he didn't answer. He just looked at me. I chalked his non-responsiveness up to crankiness. With all that he had going on, he was entitled to have a bad day every now and then. I was aware that David had diabetes. I had seen him prick his finger to check his blood-sugar level, but he had never had an episode like that during our time together. It was very scary, and I dare not to think even now about what I might have found when I got back had I lollygagged at the store.

There was another occasion when David fell at home, and that time he had to be hospitalized. "What's his name? How old is he?" asked one of the EMTs who responded to that 911 call. David, "Mr. Rivera, Mr. Rivera," one medic said in a modulated tone. David's eyes were open, but he was clearly dazed and confused.

The medics explained to David step-by-step what they were going to do. First, they were going to get him back onto the bed, let him get his bearings, and then they would transfer him to a gurney after which they would put him in the ambulance and take him to Baptist East Hospital. The protocol was calming even for me. With sirens blaring, they took off. I followed the ambulance in my car.

David got priority treatment in the emergency room because he had arrived by ambulance. In fairly short order, the EMTs completed their paperwork and handed off David to the emergency room team. Aides wheeled him into one of the glass cubicles and put him in a bed. The technicians went to work hooking him up to an IV and the machine that would monitor his pulse and heart rate.

"Thank you. Thank you," I said with deep and genuine gratitude to the two young EMTs before they left for their next run. Those young men were the angels who stood between me and a complete meltdown that day. (I wish I had gotten their names). "It's OK, ma'am," they said. "We're just doing our job. Good luck." For me, it was yet another "Jesus take the wheel" moment.

I stepped outside David's glass cubicle to call his son in Georgia. I explained that his Dad had taken a nasty fall at home and that we were at the hospital. I could see David through the glass wall and noticed that he kept sliding down in the bed. I turned my back for a few seconds, and next thing I knew, a man who was passing through the ER was yelling, "That man in there. He's having a seizure!" That man was David. ER staffers rushed passed me into the cubicle. They started working on him and calmed him for a brief time. Then suddenly, David began convulsing again. It was awful to watch. "Oh, Lord, please, please don't let him die! Please!" I heard myself saying. It was as if I was outside my own body.

The ER was busy and filled with people and yet I felt alone and helpless. I couldn't endure all those feelings by myself. I needed a friend, but who I could I call? I needed someone who would be a calming influence in the midst of the storm that was raging inside of David and inside of me watching him shaking and bouncing up and down on the hospital bed.

Clest Lanier was one of my first friends in Louisville, and we've remained tight over the decades. We've had many heart-to-hearts, and I thought that she would understand my pain. She could relate. After all, she had buried a son and knew what it was to have the awful terror crawl up inside and grab you by the throat. I don't know what plans Clest had that morning, but whatever they were, she put them aside and came to be with me. She may as well have floated in wearing wings and a halo. I fell into her arms. I didn't have to do a lot of talking; Clest just held me and let me cry.

Finally, David lapsed into a peaceful slumber inside his glass cubicle, and the ER staffers who had attended to him melted away to let him rest. His convulsions had passed, as had the hours since his arrival at Baptist East.

When Clest finally had to leave, I told her, "You're a real friend. Thank you." I walked her out and returned to my vigil. I was tempted to climb into the other bed in David's room, pull the covers over my head and rest too. I was exhausted physically, emotionally and spiritually. Mostly, however, I was afraid — afraid for David and for myself. I didn't want to begin imagining life without the love I had only just found.

David was going to be admitted to the hospital, but the process would take several more hours. I sat at the foot of David's ER bed and watched him breathing easy at last. Every now and then, he would open his eyes and call out for me. "I'm here. I'm here, Moodles." I don't believe David was aware that he was in the hospital, but feeling my presence, kisses and love whispers seemed to comfort him, and he would drift back to sleep.

My body was stiff from sitting so long in the unpadded plastic chair in David's room. As he slept, I strolled around the semi-circular ER peeking into the open doors and curtains of other rooms and cubicles. I eavesdropped on the medical staff's conversations. I eventually found refuge in the ER family room, a small, windowless space just down the hall from David's cubicle. I didn't bother to turn on the light. I just sat there luxuriating in the darkness and the momentary peace.

A few hours earlier, that little room had been occupied by the family of an elderly gent who arrived by ambulance not long after David. That's where the man's family learned that the old man was dead. The awful news wasn't likely a surprise because when the code sounded over the loudspeaker, organized chaos broke out in the ER. Doctors and other staff rushed into service visitors were shooed out of their paths. I imagined the paddles of a defibrillator being pressed hard onto the man's chest to deliver the electric shocks intended to get his heart beating again. I imagined someone monitoring his vitals and saying, "We're losing him. We're losing him." Then I imagined the moment when signs of life disappeared, and a doctor calling the time of death.

Death may be all in a day's work in the ER, but watching David sleeping fitfully inside his cubicle, I was reminded of just how swiftly the death angel can swoop in to claim its booty. There's not a thing that medicine or machines can do about it. That day in the ER was "Passover" for David. The death angel skipped over his room and had slipped into another.

It was late afternoon when the attendants finally took David upstairs to his assigned room in the ultra-modern, eight-story Baptist

Hospital East Park Tower. The tower was everything that the ER was not. The ER was tight and noisey with ambulances coming and going, people crying out in pain and the medical staff popping in and out of rooms or clustering around their computers.

The Tower's public areas looked less like a hospital and more like the lobby of a high-end hotel. It was quiet, spacious and masculine. The marble and wood floors shone like a freshly treated ice-skating rink. High-backed wing chairs, lamps and tables were organized into homey pods and the brown-and-beige color pallet was calming and matched the dark wood of the nurses' station. The windows of the patients' rooms overlooked a small park, a cluster of trees and the cityscape just beyond.

David was settled into his room and still seemed to be disoriented. His personality was in retreat. The next and final leg of his journey was about to begin. The over-sized leather recliner in the room would be my bed for the first few days of David's hospitalization.

We did not talk much and when we did, the conversation was fragmented and largely unconnected to our lives before the cancerous army was consuming more of who David was. I didn't want to be away from him. I wanted to talk with the nurses about his meds and with the doctors when they made their rounds.

Dr. Andrew J. Hart, an associate of Dr. Montes stopped in and checked on David. A few other doctors checked on him as well, but had little to say. One day, a tall, young neurosurgeon I had never seen before, came to David's room. In a brief and almost matter-of-fact tone, the doctor said that he had reviewed David's records and thought that maybe David would be a candidate for brain surgery. David couldn't comprehend but the doctor sounded crazy to me. He did not explain what the surgery would accomplish or why he thought David would be a good candidate. I called David's son to tell him what the doctor said. Levet and I agreed that it would be ridiculous, on top of everything else to subject David to some risky brain surgery.

Meanwhile, David's "angry brain tumors" were raging. He was agitated, confused, losing his balance and falling frequently. He was so sick and aggravated that he was yanking IVs out of his arms and accumulating black-and-blue bruises from his falls. He was increasingly incoherent because of the pressure being exerted by the brain tumors.

David slept a lot, but several times a day he would wake up as if a bell had gone off inside his head to signal "bathroom." He would try to get up by himself. "Wait. Wait, honey. Wait for someone to come and help you," I begged. Me telling him to wait only agitated him more. He was determined, so he would get out of bed and fall. Bam! After assessing the risks to David and I suspect a potential lawsuit, the staff moved David to a room closer to the nurses' station. His new bed had an alarm to signal when he was up and on the move. The alarm sounded several times a day, and staff came running.

After eight days in the hospital, someone decided that, as sick as he was, the time had come for David to be discharged. He needed a different level of care. Where exactly David would go was not the hospital's problem to solve. After a peer-to-peer doctor review, the insurance carriers refused to authorize David's transfer to a skilled-care facility. Faceless and nameless bureaucrats were saying, in effect, "I don't know where you're going to take him, but he's got to get out of here."

God, help us!

A hospital social worker suggested that I could care for David at home. "Maybe some of the men from your church could help," she said, and I do believe that she was serious. I was desperate for a humane solution. I was panicking. I called David's son in Georgia, explained the situation and told him to come as soon as he could.

Someone more powerful than all the paper-pushers for whom David's living, suffering and dying was of consequence, did care about David. That night at home, I fell into a restless sleep with no good answers and awoke to some force urging me to, "Call Carolyn Tandy." I had no idea why I got that instruction, but I followed it. Carolyn, at that time, was District Director for Congressman John Yarmuth, the Democrat who represents Louisville's 3rd District. Carolyn is also a friend, my sorority sister, and a member of my church. I explained to her that David was on the verge of being cast out of the hospital without a serious plan for his aftercare, and I asked, "Carolyn, can you help us?" She didn't hesitate. Within the hour, a local Hosparus Health representative showed up at the hospital. She reviewed David's paperwork, consulted with hospital staff, spoke with me and got on the phone with David's son, Levet, to discuss the options. At last, we had a rudimentary plan, the upshot of which was that we would care for David at his son's home in Georgia. Where Levet was investigating hospice services near his home in Smyrna.

Carolyn told me later that her responding to my request was a "constituent service" of Congressman Yarmuth's office. I am one of his constituents. I was aware that members of Congress can get things done that ordinary citizens can't, but it never occurred me that the help that David needed was a constituent service. Carolyn Tandy was our angel at a desperate time.

It's a wonder that Levet didn't get stopped by the police on his way to Louisville. One minute he was on the phone and the next, he appeared in the doorway of his father's hospital room. I was so relieved. Levet attempted to have a coherent conversation with his Dad, but David wasn't making a lot of sense. Before long, nature called and his son helped him get to the bathroom. But David managed to wiggle away and crashed to the floor in the bathroom. Levet was shocked. That was his first time seeing his father go down like a tree.

David spent one more night at the hospital. Levet and I went back to the condo to prepare for his father's discharge the next day. When David walked out the hospital into the daylight, he looked awful. He was unshaven, weak and so unsteady that he had to use a walker. It took some doing, but Levet finally got his Dad loaded into the car. When we got back to the condo, I went through closets gathering up coats, clothes, underwear, shoes, slippers and other necessities that I thought David would need once he got to Georgia. Our upstairs neighbors, mother and daughter, Fran and Gail Passamisi, stopped in to welcome David home and wish him well. David appeared to recognize them, but he was exhausted.

The next morning, Levet shaved his Dad and sat him in a chair inside the shower and lathered him up. David looked so innocent in the face of the gentle care he was receiving. Levet dressed his Dad and packed the car with his things. No longer self-aware, David had no idea that he was leaving the home that we had made together for probably the last time. My sweetie looked at me through the car window and waved as a child might going off to his first day of school. I stood in the driveway weeping and watching as Levet pulled away. I knew in my heart that David would never come this way again. It was one of the saddest days of my life. I walked back inside, cried some more and began organizing my affairs for my absence. I packed two suitcases and my laptop and joined David in Georgia two days later. I had no idea how long I would be gone, but I planned to be there with my man for as long as I needed to be.

Chapter 17

Georgia - (Ray Charles)

I started writing in my journal after David and I relocated to Georgia. I didn't write entries every day, nor did I realize until I transcribed the entries that I had written so much. When I was journaling, I didn't expect to write this book, and so what follows represents my raw insights and emotions in almost real time, by which I mean that I wrote either the day that or the day after different events occurred. Writing in my journal and listening to music was how I often occupied myself during the hundreds of hours that David was asleep or simply not talking.

Sometimes I wrote when I was away from David and struggling with what was going on with him and what was going on with me watching my sweetheart die a little each day. I wrote not worrying about grammar, syntax or any of that. I wrote what was in my head and my heart. I had to get what was inside of me out and onto the page.

My Journal

Friday, Oct. 31, 2014
Halloween
Levet & Shanti's House
Smyrna, Georgia

David and I are at his son's house. I couldn't maintain him in Louisville. David is fresh from 10 days in Louisville's Baptist East Hospital, where he was treated for brain tumors, including two "angry tumors," [aggressive growths] the doctor said. Hospice is working with us, and David has improved in general since coming to Georgia, but his personality has undergone a distinct shift and not for the better. He cannot comprehend how sick he is nor that I cannot take him back to Kentucky, where we don't have a support system.

I've been here since Wednesday, and I am excruciatingly sad, particularly when David lashes out at me and his son. We love him and are trying to help, but it's hard to reason with him in his condition. I realize that he's sick, but it still frustrates me when he lashes out. I'm so tired right about now. I've prayed so hard for God to show me the way. Looking forward to having dinner with my sister Georgeann and spending a little time away from this unrelenting pain and sadness, even if only for a few hours.

David isn't in physical pain, but mentally he's aware and is fighting against losing his independence. Ended up canceling dinner with G. David is agitated and wanted to eat out. Levet and I explained to David the situation: He lives here now; he cannot legally drive. This is best for him. David isn't buying any of it. Truth is that I have no skill set to deal with this situation. I literally cannot breathe. Reasoning with David seems near impossible now and because he is semi-mobile, and he's convinced that he can be self-sufficient. Aaaaargh!

Wednesday, Nov. 5, 2014
Levet & Shanti's House

Been here a week today. I miss my own bed, but, thank God, David is much improved since he left Louisville. He's not drinking. He's taking his meds and fighting to retain some semblance of his independence and dignity. He has trouble getting up and standing. When he is up, quite often he takes tentative steps. I fear for him trying to navigate the steps in Levet and Shanti's split-level home. Meanwhile, David is stubborn and won't use the plastic urinal as much as he should. So, there's lots of urine to clean up. He tries to do it himself. Sometimes, I don't believe I'll ever stop smelling urine. We all have our own urine smell. Nobody's is exactly the same. David's urine has a distinct aroma, no doubt influenced by his meds and what he's eating, which at the moment is SWEETS: Hostess chocolate cupcakes, lots of milk, and strawberry Ensure is his latest drink of choice. Also, for the last two days, my boy has been craving and downing Ritz crackers. Even so, David's comeback is a testament to his will to live. Two weeks ago, David's walking and eating like a horse, for example, just didn't seem to be in the cards.

Meanwhile, friends calling, texting and emailing really is helping me to cope in a difficult situation. Keep the prayers coming.

As I write, I've got the TV on in the guest bedroom David and I are sharing. I'm not watching but listening to Wendy Williams dishing about Tori Spelling, the actress. Why am I listening? Escapism pure and simple.

David's been quiet and sleeping most of this day. It's 4 p.m. I offered food and drink, but he said no. Very different from yesterday when David was more active. This whole situation is day-to-day, and though my heart is racing, I'm trying not to read too much into David's silence. He says he feels OK. Interestingly, nowhere on this journey so far, including chemotherapy and repeated rounds of radiation, has David ever complained of being in pain. I feel so helpless right now.

Looked at photos from just a few months ago, and David was so robust. Now, he's relatively frail and has no self-consciousness about being naked around the house.

Cancer is a monster for sure, but it cannot be said that David didn't live the life he chose. Some of those early decisions about drugs and alcohol, no doubt, are exacerbating his current struggle to live. Levet and I don't doubt for a moment that keeping David away from his "copious alcohol consumption" — Dr. Montes' words — is what's giving David the many good moments he's been able to enjoy of late. Tomorrow is another day. Hopefully, it'll be a good one.

P.S. Last night's election sucked for Democrats. I voted absentee, but to no avail. Mitch McConnell [Republican of Kentucky] was re-elected and now will be the U.S. Senate's majority leader. Look out, poor people and immigrants. It's going to be a very bumpy ride. I expect that President Obama may look much better to a lot of people now that Republicans are in charge.

Reflection: Dealing with cancer really is day-to-day. Just when you persuade yourself that things couldn't be worse, you realize that *yes*, they can be worse. Down the road on our journey, I would have given anything for David to be on his feet, demanding to be fed and able to walk, feed himself, hold his own knife, fork and spoon, binge on cupcakes and crackers, and wash them down with a big, cold glass of 2% milk. But with cancer, each day is different — watching David being overtaken and taken down by his hideous disease. I sometimes wondered, as perhaps David had as well, whether death wasn't necessarily the worse thing. At times, death may even be the blessing hoped for.

Thursday, Nov. 6, 2014
Levet & Shanti's House

David had a restless night, which means that I had a restless night. He's quiet this morning. Met up with former Louisville chum Martha Dorsey. She took me to *Pappadeaux Seafood Kitchen* for lunch. I cried my heart out. Turns out that Martha, a psychologist, lives just down the street from David's son. Go figure. Martha gave me a listening ear and offered God's wisdom to help me through. David went out for a ride with his son. Watched him from the window tottering down the walkway. I was witnessing the role reversal. The son had become the father helping the old man to walk. David placed both hands on Levet's back and walked follow-the-leader style. God, I know this is right (moving David to Atlanta) and bless this wonderful son and daughter-in-law for opening their home. Not all sons and daughters-in-law would do the same under these circumstances.

Reflection: The lesson on this day was that I needed, not just to talk, but to feel that I was really being listened to. Martha was my armor-bearer that day. I was in spiritual warfare. I was grieving, even though David was alive. He was still alive, and I was already missing him and missing us as a couple. David was still among the living, but I was already feeling unsteady, abandoned and alone as the cancer inside of him grew more insistent on settling for nothing less than David's life. My premature grief was the dress rehearsal. It was God's way, I guess, of prepping my mind, body and spirit for the physical separation just over the horizon. My mind couldn't inoculate me from the pain, but it could give me the courage to endure. I've come to equate my state of mind that day to how phlebotomists, before drawing blood, usually warn us that the needle's prick is going to hurt. The protocol apparently is that anticipating pain makes its coming just a little easier to endure.

Friday, Nov. 7, 2014
Levet & Shanti's House

Overnight was horrific. David was a bear, a real butt head. Potty break after potty break and a tumble off the bed. Levet had a helluva time getting his father up off the floor. God, take care of Levet's back and carry us all through David's demands, gently put as, "When you get the chance, can you get me—?" Cereal and milk once at 12:30 a.m. and again at 3:15 a.m. Around 7:15 a.m., it was "coffee *por favor*." How do I know the times? I checked. Exhausted.

Incredible dream about authorities wanting to remove a child from his family.

Don't understand the dream, just that for whatever reason, in it some of my sorors came from New York City to help. Didn't find out what happened to the child, but my friends went out to dinner, and I couldn't connect with them by cellphone. Kept trying, but it wouldn't work. Crazy dream. Crazy life right now.

Levet said a funny thing this a.m. because his sleep had been interrupted too. Said he heard noises in the middle of the night, went to the kitchen and found David taking a knife to get the box open to eat a cake Levet's mother-in-law brought over the night before. David was butt naked, Levet said, and was busily hacking away trying to get to that cake. Anyhow, Levet looked at me and said, "Your pardon is coming soon" and to be honest, at times this journey does feel like prison. Whew!

Reflection: Levet's recounting of his Dad, in the dining room in the middle of the night, hacking away at the cakebox was poignant. To be perfectly honest, the re-telling brought a moment of comic relief, a shared laugh between David's son and me, on a journey that was becoming increasingly difficult and unpredictable. The blessing, I suppose, is that David seemed unaware that his serious attempt to get at a sweet that he craved was a joke to us. As we suffered watching David veer from lucid to just nuts, he was being protected by a mind corrupted by the "babies," the lay term David's oncologist used for the smaller tumors that have broken from their Mama and Papa cancer cells in David's lungs. That less than sophisticated terminology actually helped me to imagine what was happening to David. There were these baby cancer cells eager to move out on their own, eager to leave their parents' nest and establish independent colonies in the body of their host, in this case, eager to set up shop in David's brain. The radiation treatments slowed them down, but only for a while. They may be babies, but they were strong.

Monday, Nov. 10, 2014
Jackson, Mississippi

Arrived here yesterday for the Trotter Group (African American columnists) meeting at Jackson State University. Wasn't planning to attend, but my dear friend DeWayne Wickham from Morgan State University urged me to come, effectively for respite care. Indeed, "Wick" slipped me $200 to help underwrite my expenses. He is indeed my friend.

Once I settled in at the Hilton Garden Inn Hotel Downtown, I called back to Smyrna and the David report was pretty good. David slept a lot but did eat a chicken pot pie. He's barely been eating "real" food, just sweets: Hostess chocolate cupcakes, gallons of milk and the strawberry Ensure.

David is a wonder, a true ghetto survivor. At 66, he's already outlived many of our childhood friends who took the same journey as David — addictions to drugs, alcohol and cigarettes. David abandoned hard drugs decades ago and cigarettes about three and-a-half years ago, which as it turns out, was too late to avoid lung cancer. David still loves a good joint though, and alcohol, particularly brandy, in "copious" amounts, as his oncologist Ignacio Montes wrote in his notes. David is one of those quiet drinkers. He sips all day and never appears to be drunk. I would never have tolerated a raving drunk.

I'm a total teetotaler and intend to live forever alcohol- and drug-free. Thank you, Jesus and Daddy! I'm "addicted" to other things: good conversation, good books, good friends and my family. I thank God for all of them. Just thinking about them gives me strength for this journey. As he often is, Wickham is right. Being with my journalist family is invigorating me. Rochelle Riley, a Detroit newspaper columnist, gave me a tight, warm hug, an expression of sisterly concern. Yeah, I needed these few days to be *loved on* by colleagues I've known for years.

This is my first "real" time in Mississippi, [I had driven through it years before] and the road sign, Meridian, for example, conjures up "Civil Rights Movement," thoughts of Emmitt Till, Fannie Lou Hamer, Medgar Evers, Muhammad Kenyatta, Ralph Featherstone and other brave legends who came here to Mississippi as young people to bravely battle racism and segregation. They were forever changed, and they changed the world.

Chatted with a lovely Jackson State mass communications major whom I hoped would appreciate the historical irony of her journey from Chicago to Mississippi, but she showed no sign of recognition. I specifically asked about her family's reaction to her choosing this school in this place. Lovely child, really, but no sign of a political understanding of this career she's about to embark on. She's not as "fluffy" as many young African Americans, and so she has potential. With the right educational experiences, she could become more than just another pretty face in the media. God knows we've got enough of that.

Reflection: Stepping out, even briefly, from the pain and sadness of watching David dying a little each day, was a good thing, though admittedly I felt guilty for taking a few days to catch my breath and, for a brief time, to get back to my old life before the thief of a terminal illness crept in and stole my joy of having found love again when I didn't expect it.

Tuesday Nov. 11, 2014
Jackson, Mississippi

Last day of Trotter meeting. It's been a long day but exceptional in terms of content and camaraderie. Civil rights tour: Medgar Evers' home, the first public school for African Americans in the state and the Council of Federated Organizations (COFO) office where we had lunch and met with local NAACP activists. I called Mae Jackson and Joyce Ladner to talk about me, 50 years later, being in some of the same places where my heroes Fannie Lou Hamer, Bob Moses, Joyce and her sister, Dorie Ladner, Ralph Featherstone, as well as James Chaney, Andrew Goodman and Michael "Mickey" Schwerner, worked hard to help us get free.

Chaney, Goodman and Schwerner paid with their lives. It was awesome and emotional. This tour brought back a flood of emotions and new insights.

Called back to Georgia to check on David. He fell again and as instructed by hospice, Levet called the Smyrna fire department to help get his dad off the floor. Hospice has a brought a hospital bed and set it up in the living room. Hospice staff seem not to believe, as I do, that David may have suffered a stroke that has severely weakened his right side. In some ways, having the hospital bed is better for David because he won't be consigned to lying flat, and with the sidebars up, the risk of him falling at Levet's is diminished,

Oh, David! And why is my left hand going numb while I'm writing this?

This journey is horrific. God bless us all.

Wednesday, Nov. 12, 2014
Hartsfield-Jackson Airport
Atlanta, Georgia

Back in the ATL from Mississippi and waiting for Levet to pick me up. Can't wait to see David and to kiss and hug him. It's one thing to be told how David's doing and another to see for myself. I am unrelentingly sad and feeling helpless, but as Sherrie Lyons, a long-time Louisville friend, said, "This is the process." I'm going to hold out faint hope at least that David will rally one more time. I'm learning not to count him out. When I'm most despaired, he surprises me.

Reflection: Do I dare believe that David can pull back from the brink? He's strong. He's resilient. He's Don Pepe. Don DaVid. He's overcome other challenges in his life. Why not cancer? Hope is eternal because at the end of the day, it's not doctors, it's not hospice, but God who will have the final say. Live David. Live!

Friday, Nov. 14, 2014
Levet & Shanti's House
Smyrna, Georgia

Just seven days ago, David was walking, talking and quite frankly, driving us all a little nuts. Today and yesterday, he slept for hours, and now I'm sitting, listening to and watching him breathe. I feel peace as healing music plays. When he is awake, my David is quiet, and his speech is labored and low. My soldier is still putting up a fight, but this long struggle is taking a toll. The blessing is that David doesn't appear to be in pain. That's God's mercy.

I really enjoy my quiet moments talking with Levet. I realize that he has good reason to have issues with his Dad. They likely will go unresolved. However, the love and compassion that he's showing for his father melts my heart.

David's granddaughter, Aryanna, is a loving, sensitive and compassionate child. She's nine — about to be 10 in a few weeks, and it was beautiful last night watching her spoon feeding her grandpa ice cream and giving him gooey cookies.

Levet cooked jambalaya last night, and it was simply delicious.

God, you are merciful, and I don't know how we would make it without you. "Yea, though I walk through the valley in the shadow of death I will fear no evil: for thou art with me." [Psalm 23. King James Version] What a journey this is. God touch David.

Reflection: I am reminded that my David shares his name, not just with his father, but also with a great King named David, who as a child was a shepherd, and though he became a king, never forgot his humble roots and how God blessed him. As a child, he defeated a giant named Goliath and saved his people from certain slaughter. And God loved David and blessed and forgave him when he fell from Grace. God gifted David with wisdom and the ability to write words that centuries after his death people the world over would recite, especially the 23rd Psalm. I learned the 23rd Psalm as a child, and I've recited it hundreds of time. On this night, those words comfort me. It gives me peace just to know that God didn't only love King David, but my David too.

Sunday, Nov. 16, 2014
Wellstar Community Hospicee
Tranquility @ Cobb
Austell, Georgia

It's been an eventful day. It's the day of realization that Levet, Shanti and I cannot properly or safely care for David at home. Levet's back has given out, and he's being treated for it. Levet called this morning for respite care for his Dad, but a preliminary assessment indicates that, just as the home hospice nurse said, David needs "a lot of care" and so rather than respite care (five days max) David has been admitted as an in-patient, which is covered by his insurance and Medicare.

David has been sleeping most of the day. He's unable to stand or walk. He could get well enough to go back home to Levet and Shanti's house. Only God knows, but he also could deteriorate further and quickly, which means that he either stays here at Tranquility or another facility. I pray that he will be allowed to stay here. It's beautiful and comfortable, and the staff already has shown great kindness and compassion.

The highlight of the day was a visit by David's friend Lawrence, his wife, Pam Roy, and his friend Ibin Muhammad. The guys really stepped up in helping us to prepare David for his transfer to hospice. God has opened every door when I've felt afraid.

I am settling in for the night in David's room, H8. I am relieved just knowing that David is safe in this place. Everybody can now get a little rest. Thank you, God.

Reflection: A day of realization. A Day of Reckoning. Realizing and reckoning that the journey is getting tougher. I took a photo of Lawrence and Ibin helping to clean up David in the hospital bed at his son's house. In the photo, each old friend has one of

David's arms, and all three are smiling, when the truth is that, other than David, all of us in the living room are crying on the inside. We're pretending to be upbeat for David's sake. I look at that photo, and tears press against the back of my eyes because in that moment, big, strong, powerful David seemed so childlike, so innocent, and so blessedly unaware that in a few hours he would be relocated from the familiar surroundings of his son's home to the hospice. Two EMS workers loaded David onto a stretcher, rolled him down the gentle slope of the walkway of his son's home and slid him into the ambulance. I followed them through winding back streets to the hospice, a lovely one-floor building on the grounds of Cobb County Hospital. My heart aches, as I relive what would be David's last day in our care at home.

I picked up a pamphlet at the hospice titled, "When the Time Comes: A Caregiver's Guide." The opening paragraph said in part, "Dying is a natural part of life, but many people do not have experience caring for someone during the dying process and find themselves navigating new and unfamiliar territory. It is not uncommon to experience a range of emotions and a sense of uncertainty. At times you may feel that you are on a roller coaster, not knowing what to expect next."

Every death and every journey to death is individual, but the signs of impending death and the up-one-day, down-the-next emotions experienced by loved ones of the dying are nearly universal. This pamphlet and other handouts that I perused were difficult and emotional to read, but crucial to my understanding of what was happening to David, to me, his son and all who loved him and were regretting that we were about to lose him. We don't know the day or the hour, only that he is going to die, and nothing any of us can do will stop or slow down the process. What we can do, however, is to pray and let David know that we love him, wish he could stay, but if he has to go, that the end be painless and peaceful.

Monday, Nov. 17, 2014
Wellstar Community Hospice
Tranquility @ Cobb

It's only 1:45 a.m., but it feels like 3 o'clock in the morning. I've been trying to sleep on the pull-out sofa in David's room, but I can't resist watching him breathe in and out, a steady rhythm, sometimes deep, sometimes shallow, I was struck by how, for better than five minutes, David's left hand was elevated and trembling as if he was holding something back. He seemed to be struggling against it.

Suddenly, he woke up and said, "Hi, Moo-Moo," his pet name for me.

"How are you feeling?" I asked, and he said, "Tired," though he had been sleeping for most of the day.

I've read the booklet, "When the Time Comes: A Caregivers Guide" about what to expect when someone is dying and what to do when certain behaviors change, when appetite changes and when body functions change.

David is already exhibiting some signs, but I can feel him fighting.

When he's sleeping, I wonder if he's dreaming and about what. I notice that he's starting to yawn a lot.

David hasn't eaten since yesterday morning, but unlike at home, he's not asking for cupcakes, Ensure, a jelly doughnut or a Pepsi.

This facility is aptly named. It is Tranquil, and I love having this quiet time for David and for myself. Still, it feels later than it is. Maybe it's because I went to bed early — in the middle of my favorite Sunday night TV show — "The Good Wife."

Give us — David and I — this day!

Tuesday, Nov. 18, 2014
Wellstar Community Hospice
Tranquility @ Cobb

Today is quiet. David has slept the entire day, other than early this morning when I fed him small portions of egg with spinach, bacon, a waffle with syrup, followed by coffee, Diet Coke (he requested) and chocolate-covered wafers, orange juice and water. Sounds like a lot, but the portions were tiny.

Since then, he has slept through a diaper change, a big bowel movement clean-up, a visit by Dr. Irene to relieve pressure on his brain by increasing his steroid medication a few milligrams.

David finally woke up about 10 p.m. He ate a shaved ice treat given by a nurse and drank two small containers of juice. He speaks when spoken to but doesn't initiate conversations, and he never speaks more than a few words. He did perk up and say the Spanish word for shaved-ice treats, *piragua*. He was reacting to me telling the nurse the story that David shared with me about his grandfather Meliton, beloved by David, making him a *piragua* cart when David was a boy from which David sold flavored shaved ice.

I turned the TV to "Animal Planet," one of David's favorite channels. He stayed awake. His eyes were fixed on the TV, but David was silent. He just stared, and I wasn't sure he was comprehending what he was watching. I remembered when my Mom, on her cancer journey, would similarly lapse into this same sort of silence. Is this the sign of disconnecting from the world that I read about?

Touching Moments Today:

David taking my hand, putting it to his lips and kissing it.

David puckering up to kiss me whenever I brushed up against his face.

David waving to me in the middle of the night to assure me that he's awake.

David hearing me crunch on a potato chip and wordlessly sticking his hand out repeatedly for me to give him one chip, then another, another and so forth.

David's silence, to be honest, is unnerving. I fear what it signals.

Levet stayed home to tend to his back, which he injured trying to pick David up after a fall, and Shanti is cleaning house in preparation for Levet's mom, Juanita, and her sister, Margie, flying in from New York to see about Levet, Juanita's baby boy. They will stay until the day after Thanksgiving. It's going to be crowded at Levet's and Shanti's, so I will stay here at the hospice with David, and depending on the circumstances, I will move either to the home of my nephew Darnell Winston and his wife, Tamika, in Buford or to Inetta Jackson's in Lithonia to be with her cousin Vanessa Williams while she's visiting for the holiday.

Note to self: Levet needs to get the health directive signed and notarized a.s.a.p. while his Dad is still able to sign his name. [David was able to sign it.]

It's 10:51 p.m. I'm out.

Wednesday, Nov. 19, 2014
Wellstar Community Hospice
Tranquility @ Cobb

A nurse spoke with David's sister Bennie and David's daughter, Liza, today by phone. She didn't sugarcoat David's prognosis. "No, he will not get better," she explained. Matter of fact, he will continue to deteriorate, "but we will keep him comfortable and pain-free."

Bennie and Liza wept. I understand. I cry a little every day.

Today may be the day that removes from them deniability as to how much David's cancer has progressed. I'm looking at him every day and every night, and even I would wish I could deny what my eyes, my heart and my spirit are shouting at me. The similarities between David's, my mom's and my dad's journeys dying from the complications due to lung cancer that has spread, are undeniable. One difference, however, is that my Dad, until very late in his illness, still had a twinkle in his eyes. That's not true for my mom and David. Maybe that's due to the locations of their brain tumors, and in particular the part of the brain that controls emotions.

Today, for the first time, when I told David I loved him, he didn't answer. I hope that's because, though he seems to be awake, he really is asleep. I'll try again later today. Right now, I'm off to Levet's to pick up my belongings. He and Shanti need their guest room for his mother and her sister.

David had visitors today: Juanita (Levet's mother), Margie (her sister), Levet and Shanti and their daughter, Aryanna. He slept much of the day but was awake and especially more alert when Aryanna, his granddaughter, came near his bed. We ate Jamaican food — oxtails, cabbage, peas and rice. Delicious! David could not eat it.

When Levet and the family left, David grew quiet again, not answering most questions, staring at nothing and incessantly picking at and pulling at his gown and sheets.

This is the process. David's slowly disconnecting. Less and less does he say, "I love you too, Moo-Moo," and less and less does he respond to my affectionate, "I love you, Moodles."

Well, it's 11:20 p.m. and I'm crawling into bed, the hard, narrow couch in David's hospice room.

Thursday, Nov. 20, 2014
Wellstar Community Hospice
Tranquility @ Cobb

A quiet day for David. I played some of his favorite songs by Cecilia Cruz, Jimmy Sabater, Ibrahim Ferrer, Buena Vista Social Club and Cheo Feliciano. David's sister Bennie said David used to sing

Feliciano's "Amada Mĺia," all the time. David listened to that song with his eyes closed as if reminiscing. I can't say what he's thinking, or even if he is thinking, but it feels as if he is. When I asked what the title meant, David, who appeared to be asleep piped up to say, "My Beloved." These hours of near-silence have a sad yet uplifting impact. Sometimes, I just sit and look at David staring but seeming to be looking at nothing. This is a sad but ethereal experience I shall not soon forget and more so because in my journal I am making note of the small things that go into making the big whole.

David's still handsome in his illness, though "Prince Hakim" has definitely left the building. If he does make demands in this phase, they are small: a wave to signal more Ensure or more ice drinks that he really seems to like. No demands now to go home to Kentucky or for a drink or a joint. Those things have receded into a life that David has left behind. No more frantic dialing to reach the "smoke man."

We're now listening to another favorite singer of David and mine's, the Afro-Portuguese songstress Sarah Tavares. No matter that we don't understand Portuguese, the feelings in her music — joy, sadness, loneliness —- are universal. Indeed, the music might be less impactful if we understood the words.

I don't believe I've ever loved David more than now as I watch him facing death quietly, contemplatively and sweetly. I'm blown away by his peace. Nevertheless, it still is true that God has the final say.

Saturday, Nov. 22, 2014
Wellstar Community Hospice
Tranquility @ Cobb

Today is my sister Georgeann's birthday. She's 59. Mom and Dad's youngest of three isn't so young any more.

Meanwhile, I'm here with David and seeing him imprisoned in a body that's failing. His right side, for all practical purposes, is paralyzed, and his left side is severely weakened. I'm watching

David at war with his cancer that is taking him down, that has robbed him of memory and increasingly robbed him of speech. My poor David is desperately wanting but not accepting that he cannot get out of bed, cannot wash himself, brush his teeth or walk on his own. This helplessness is gruesome for someone who loved to walk anytime he wanted to.

What's he thinking in the deathly silence of this single room that we've been sharing for six days? The nurse insists that though David isn't speaking very much, he's "doing a lot of work," she said, reflecting on his life. Regrets?

Every now and then, I think that I detect tears when I see his son. Levet is big and strong as his dad once was. He has a family but is probably having difficulty confronting the harsh reality that his dad is a very sick man. I believe this because Levet actually seems to think that his dad is capable of playing chess on our I-Pad. He would set up the game on the tablet and set it in front of David, who would poke at the screen as if he were playing.

I'm lying here on the narrow couch watching David struggling against his bed covers that may feel to him as if he's been buried alive. A room with a view is what David and I have here at hospice. French doors open onto a small cement patio outfitted with weather-beaten lawn chairs and a small table. The grassy courtyard is strewn with fallen needles and leaves from the tall Georgia pines and other trees. I've never been good with identifying species of trees and plants. Blame my New York City upbringing.

We're listening to popular instrumentals on David's TV that remind me of the old black-and-white movies that I loved when I was kid. Right now, the song playing is "I'll Be Seeing You," and I'm thinking how appropriate it is for this moment. It's utterly peaceful here, and it's amazing how this one room and bath have become the center of our universe — just David, I, the music and the brown fallen needles and leaves from the tall trees outside. Clearly, we Americans could live in a lot less space than we do and be happy. When I was at Harvard back in 1991, I lived in two small rooms and was perfectly happy for nine months.

And there's David filling up that narrow hospital bed off in another world — the world of the dying, where I imagine kinks get worked out. When God will finally tell David "come home to me and rest," I do not know, but from what I can see, the journey will be hard on us all.

Sunday, Nov. 23, 2014
Wellstar Community Hospice
Tranquility@Cobb

David had a great day — made a fist like Ali when he got sick of me putting his hospital gown on after he kept pulling it off, but I had to giggle when he looked at me and said, "I want to have sex with you" and then promptly fell back to sleep. He's still in there!

Georgeann and Nancy visited, and David was perhaps the most animated he's been since arriving here by ambulance last Sunday. His friend Lawrence Roy came yesterday. Levet came last night. David's speech was better today than most days. It's 11 p.m., another tranquil evening @ Tranquility. I pray that David will be allowed to stay here a little longer. This is a peaceful, clean and safe place for him and for me. God keeps coming through for us. He will, one way or the other. He reigns. Angels watching over David: Levet; Shanti; Aryanna; all the Rivera sisters; David's daughter, Liza; granddaughter, Clachelle, and me. Do your thing, God.

Monday, Nov. 24, 2014
Wellstar Community Hospice
Tranquility @ Cobb

Today is quite likely the last that I will sleep in the same room as David. Looks like tomorrow, he will transfer from Tranquility, which provides short-term care, to a Catholic-run hospice in Atlanta for long-term care. Medicare and his insurance would only pay for a limited stay. He's resting comfortably, largely unaware.

I believe that he will be moving for the fifth time since mid-October: from our house to Baptist East; back to our house, then to Levet's house in Smyrna, from Levet's house to Tranquility and now to Our Lady of Perpetual Help Home, where he apparently will be in a semi-private room with specified visiting hours. It is said that Our Lady is a wonderful facility though I seriously doubt it will be as lovely as Tranquility. I suppose I should be grateful to have had seven nights of David all to myself. Our Lady may be David's last stop on this side.

Tuesday, Nov. 25, 2014
Wellstar Community Hospice
Tranquility @ Cobb

Surprise! We are here for another night. Sitting here with David listening to smooth jazz. We are in retreat. Our world now is this room with a door with no lock. Staff and volunteers come in and out at will to talk, pray, change, clean up and turn David so that his skin doesn't break from laying in the same position too long. David, again out of the blue, asks me, "Why are you so good to me?" Sometimes he just stares at me. I ask why, and today he said, "Because I have nothing else to do."

Whomever said these are precious moments couldn't be more right. In the new place, a semi-private room won't afford us this kind of quiet and intimacy. I am so enjoying this tranquility and throughout the day touching base with the world via cell phone and the internet. The facility has been decorated for Christmas — trees, lights, snowmen, garland etc. — but I am quietly thinking that it's Christ who rules and who has positioned David and me to be together for a time such as this.

It's shift change at the facility, and each shift brings a different vibe. The lavender that the caretaker put on David smells so good, and it's calming. God bless the certified nursing assistants here at

Tranquility. Their compassion is much needed and greatly appreciated as David and I take this journey together. Only God can say when I must get off the train and let David travel to his final destination without me. Obviously, I too will have to travel the last mile with a companion not seeable with human eyes.

Wednesday, Nov. 26, 2014
Our Lady of Perpetual Help Home
Atlanta, Georgia

David was transferred from Tranquility, an upscale hospice, to this Catholic-run facility. No private rooms. Everything is very clean; food is excellent and the environment is spartan. This place is absolutely *free.* No insurance plans, Social Security, Medicare or Medicaid are accepted here. The facility will not accept money from patients or patients' families. Amazing in our capitalist society. I'm told food is prepared by outside chef volunteers. Other patients are in David's room, but it is spacious with a huge window. The hospice abuts Atlanta's Turner Field, home to the Atlanta Braves baseball team.

Our Lady is just so much better than I expected. It's clean, it smells good, and male nurses are caring for David. Rather than a hospital gown, David's wearing good-looking pajamas.

Levet; Aryanna; Levet's mom, Juanita; and her sister, Margie, left a half hour ago to get ready for their Thanksgiving dinner. Our Lady has visiting hours, so I can't stay overnight with David. When I leave here, I'm heading to Lithonia to spend the evening with my friend *the* Vanessa Williams and her sister Inetta.

Thursday, Nov. 27, 2014
Thanksgiving
Darnell & Tamika's House
Buford, Georgia

Lord, I'm still here in Georgia accumulating miles on my car, but despite my heavy heart, this is a wonderful Thanksgiving. I had a wonderful morning in Lithonia with Vanessa, Inetta and Iyanna, Inetta's daughter. Spent the night, washed clothes, ate a slice of Vanessa's pound cake and had a cup of coffee and conversation. Said so long and drove back to Our Lady to sit with David.

It was a wonderful day at the hospice. David was gussied up in somebody's clothes, and he looked good. His caretakers sat him up in a recliner. Bravo. He was out of bed for the first time in days. A special family Thanksgiving meal had been prepared, and we gathered, patients and families, in a large space in the lower level. David was half asleep but hearing everything and being buoyed by the presence of his family: Levet, Shanti, Aryanna, Juanita, Margie and me.

He's puckered up for kisses and whispered, "I love you" in response to our hugs. Levet, Aryanna and I took turns feeding him small portions. He was happy, and the food was delicious — compliments of a chef from Cameroon who said he went to cooking school in France. Levet and Margie packed up a couple of take-out plates. As I said, it was wonderful. David sat for more than an hour in the dayroom. Levet FaceTimed David's sister Millie. She was so happy to see her brother.

David was sleeping comfortably when I left him around 4. I drove about 40 miles northeast out of Atlanta to have dinner with my sister Georgeann; my niece Tinisha and her beau, Lorenzo Martin aka Ty; my nephew Darnell and his family; Darnell's best friend, Herb Magwood; and Herb's cousin Lavolta Allen and their families. I'm currently resting comfortably at Darnell and Tamika's home.

My nephew Larry called from New York to check on me. "I love you Aunt Betty," he said. "Me and Poodie (the nickname I gave Darnell when he was a baby) love you." My heart melted. My nephews are good men and fathers. Mommy and Daddy must be smiling from heaven. My friend Rev. Dianne Brown, just prayed for me over the telephone. I feel good.

Sunday, Nov. 30, 2014
Cousin Gloria's House
Fairburn, Georgia

Today, I woke to the sound of an old-fashioned, round-faced wall clock with a red second hand sounding like a beating human heart. I'm in a bedroom at Gloria's house. She's my Philadelphia cousin, my godmother Annie's niece with whom I spent many summers in her father's house in West Philadelphia. Since last month, I have slept in beds in Smryna, Lithonia, Riverdale, Fairburn and 10 days on a pullout couch in David's hospice room in Austell. Wish I could say like the old gospel song, "Ain't no ways tired," but I am. This is what I have to do to stay on this journey with my soulmate.

Speaking of David, I sat with him about six hours yesterday. He slept most of the time, except for a brief stint when I was able to feed him a little bit of chicken salad, tomato soup, banana pudding and a glass of creamy strawberry Boost. While he slept, I read on my computer and read more of Chimamanda Ngozi Adichie's novel, "Americanah."

I'm really missing David being with me in the usual way: sleeping next to me, talking about whatever and making me crazy with requests for Hostess chocolate cupcakes, strawberry Ensure and cookies. I realize that he will never be in my kitchen again making roast pork Puerto Rican style, stirring up arroz con gandules (rice with pigeon peas) and making batches of coquito ("little coconut" — a milky, spiked beverage similar to eggnog) to give as Christmas presents. David was no angel; he drank much too much, but I miss my Moodles sitting in his man cave at the condo playing chess on his computer, listening to salsa or Santeria music surrounded by remnants of half-smoked joints.

Had a nice breakfast with Gloria before she went off to church. What a journey this is. God, you know what this day holds. I don't, but whatever, hold me close and keep your arms around David, all of his family and mine.

Going to get dressed, pick up Georgeann at her house and head back to Our Lady to sit with David.

Tuesday, Dec. 2, 2014
Our Lady of Perpetual Help Home

"He's still in there," the male nurse said in response to my inquiry about David's blank stare in which he never looks at me. He did connect, however, when I asked him for a kiss and to squeeze my hand with his hand on his good side. The pucker and the squeeze were faint, but what's important is that he heard me.

David had other company yesterday. Donald Robinson (a family friend from Louisville) visited for two hours. He was in Atlanta on business. David was less responsive today, but Donald and I felt that David was aware of Donald's presence. Took a few photos of Donald with David and Levet with David. Yesterday, David was wearing a sunny yellow sweater that complimented his skin. Today he's wearing a red sweater. When I arrived, his eyes were closed, and he was wearing headphones to listen to his personal TV to keep him stimulated.

Took Gloria to Ruby Tuesday for dinner last night to celebrate her birthday. The meal was delicious, but the conversation about family and life was wonderful. When we were young women and Gloria still lived in Philly and I still lived in New York, she and I got in the habit of writing letters back and forth. We went deep. For years, I kept a shoebox of Gloria's letters. She had beautiful penmanship and still does.

When I got to OLPH, one of David's roommates seemed to be having a tough day, He was a white guy whom we nicknamed "Hot Wheels" because he would zip up and down the halls, and sometimes outside, in a wheelchair. He's gagging and coughing, and he keeps apologizing. He just said that he should be in a single room because he's throwing up and making other people sick. He's kept the curtain closed around his bed.

Meanwhile, David is reflexively trembling on his left side and putting his hand on his head. Wish I could speak with Dr. Montes back in Louisville to get a sense of what's going on. I think I'll call him. I left a message. David is on a natural journey, no extreme treatments or meds, only steroids and morphine when he needs it, but David never complains that he's hurting or feeling stress. This is palliative care. It's quite amazing that during this entire journey I've never heard David complain of pain of any significance, or even of nausea. He's a wonder.

Tuesday, Dec. 2, 2014
Cousin Gloria's House
Fairburn, Georgia

It's 12:30 a.m. I'm resting in one of Gloria's guest bedrooms listening to the wall clock with the second hand that grates against the clock's cardboard face. Every second puts me in the mind of a loud heartbeat, and I'm reminded of how David's life is ticking away. It's true of all our lives, but we don't all have incurable cancer. So, David's death appears most imminent and urgent.

December 3, 2014
Our Lady of Perpetual Help Home

For the first time since David's arrival at Our Lady of Perpetual Help Home a week ago, I've seen a doctor examine him, nothing deep, just feeling him lightly and shining a light into David's staring eyes that look but seem not to see. The elderly doctor, John Read, walking with a cane, is accompanied by a nun, Sister Mae Fung Koo, who appears to be in charge of the floor and who spoke loudly calling David's name. He responded, not to her words, but to the authoritative sound.

"I speak only in probabilities," Dr. Read told me after stepping out of David's earshot. He reminded me of the kind of care David will receive.

"We keep them comfortable," he explained. Levet and I do understand that extraordinary care — chemo and radiation, for example, is not offered at Our Lady. Anyhow, David's been there and done that already, and now in effect he is dying naturally. "The probability is one month, maybe less, but I've been wrong before," said the doctor, who wasn't unfriendly, but just wasn't warm, fuzzy or chatty. He had other patients to see.

I left Our Lady to meet my sister Georgeann and take her to dinner at Annie Laura's Soul Food Kitchen in Riverdale. G listened sympathetically when I told her what the doctor said. Dropped her back at home and drove back to Gloria's house.

Thursday, Dec. 4, 2014
Our Lady of Perpetual Help Home

A beautiful day. The sun is out. It's warm, and I'm here with David. Gloria sent me off with a wonderful breakfast, prayer and conversation. Gloria had washed, dried, folded my clothes and helped me load up my car. I'm going to Smyrna tonight to spend time with the Riveras: Levet, Shanti and Aryanna. First, I'm off to OLPH. David is resting but is making more noise than he has in days. He's sighing and making other sounds, not snoring, but soft sounds as if he's soothing himself. Aaaah! He's not responding, but I believe he hears my voice. These are the sounds of peace.

Meanwhile, OLPH is being converted into a Christmas wonderland. The halls are decorated. The room doors are decorated.

The workers are hanging wreaths, and a life-sized manger scene sits outside. It's not quite done yet, but I'll take a photo.

I had a wonderful conversation with the social worker, Ellen Slack. Blessedly, Levet was here this morning, and Ellen and he had a conversation too, she said. I'm glad for that because Levet isn't verbalizing it, but I know he's having a tough time. He has to be.

Oh, and let me not forget that Dr. Montes called me back yesterday. I felt that David had a special bond with his first oncologist. He always seemed committed to David beyond the usual patient care. I told him where we were and what was happening. He listened, though clearly none of what I was saying was unfamiliar to him.

I was struck by the fact that before asking about David, Dr. Montes asked about my knee replacement. He remembered. I told him my truth. I had been so invested in David's journey that I haven't thought much about my own health. My sense always has been that I have time, but David doesn't. Truth is that we're all on God's calendar.

Saturday, Dec. 6, 2014
Our Lady of Perpetual Help Home

Started out a bluesy Saturday at the Rivera house. Levet & Shanti were listening to the blues music of Clarence Carter, Albert King, B.B. King and then moved on to Sly and the Family Stone, the Whispers etal. Levet cooked breakfast: eggs, pancakes and bacon. Mmmmm.

Later, we all went to OLPH, where David was having a good day too. His eyes are open. He's more alert, speaking a bit but hearing everything. Aryanna has a particularly good effect on David. He flashed her a crooked smile and gave her a robust kiss. Lord, give us this day. A group of Filipino Christmas carolers stopped and sang to patients in every room at OLPH. They sang "Feliz Navidad" (Merry Christmas) at Levet's request, and David reacted positively. I captured the scene on my iPad. Thank God from whom all blessings flow. It's 6 p.m., and David has eaten some of a pureed something or the other. He ate a whole container of apple sauce and drank a good portion of juice. He's drifting off to sleep.

Monday, Dec. 8, 2014
Our Lady of Perpetual Help Home

Yesterday was eventful at OLPH. More visitors than I've ever seen. Maybe because St. Nick came to visit the patients. The nuns were all aflutter passing out homemade cookies, punch and teddy bears. David got a brown one. Sweet cousin Gloria came and sat with David and me. We ate cold spaghetti from her church. Aryanna, Shanti and Levet missed St. Nick but found him upstairs on the female patients' floor. David had moments of wakefulness, and as always, he was particularly responsive to his Aryanna. I'm sure he would be the same if Clachelle, his oldest granddaughter, and his daughter, Liza, were here.

It's 2:50 p.m., and David just opened his eyes, focused on me and said, "Hi, Moo Moo." He said something else that I couldn't make out. I thank God for small moments such as this when I know that he knows that I'm here.

Last night, I treated Gloria to Southern Buffett, for dinner. And lest I forget, I had a wonderful time Saturday at my friend Cynthia Williams' annual holiday gathering of women at her gorgeous home in Snellville, Georgia. I took advantage of the masseur, Clinton, who had set up shop in the lower level of Cynthia's home. The hour-long massage did me a world of good.

The gathered women, including Santa Wright, a friend from Louisville, shared our aspirations, situations, expectations and what we wanted to leave behind in 2014. We cried. We prayed. Besides Cynthia and Santa, all the women were strangers to me. They laid hands on me, and Cynthia, she of the beautiful voice, sang a few selections from her Christmas CD. I especially loved an original, "Grateful." I bought two CDs, one for me and one for Gloria, who is being the best hostess to me.

I learned last night that my friend Marilyn Milloy's husband died yesterday. (Marilyn is a fellow journalist I know through NABJ.) She's been on a journey similar to mine. God bless my friend and her family. Cancer doesn't respect age, race or class. It's a monster. I pray that one day there will be a cure. Gloria and I watched a "60 Minutes" segment about a South African doctor of Asian descent doing research that he hopes will lead to cancer being a treatable disease. I won't live to see it, but that would be a miracle.

Back at OLPH, David's roommate "Hot Wheels" is having a very difficult time. He's on oxygen and sometimes cries for help. I am grateful that David seems oblivious to the drama and is breathing on his own. God is merciful.

I arrived in Georgia Oct. 29. Wednesday will be six weeks. I miss home, but I'm where I need and want to be, near David. I took a lot of calls from friends today — from Louisville, Everett Todd, Marita Willis, and Margie Duvall, as well as LaVerne Vance from Maryland, and Kathy Skiba, a Nieman classmate from Virginia.

I fed David. He drank all of his juice. He's drifting off listening to some of his favorite music: "Balance" by Sarah Tavares. David and "Hot Wheels" are the only two patients in the room at the moment. The Christmas tree in the room is so pretty with its colored lights. There's a small manger scene and Frosty the Snowman on the window sill. A paper bell hangs on a nail over David's bed. It's adorned with a cardinal and the words, "Celebrate the Wonder of Christmas." I'm celebrating the wonder of God in directing us to this wonderful, remarkable place staffed by wonderful people —- the nuns and the male caregivers. I'm so grateful.

Tuesday, Dec. 9, 2014
Our Lady of Perpetual Help Home

This is an exceptionally good day. David's eyes have been wide open. He's talking, seems to be comprehending and even holding his own juice cup up to his mouth to drink. He's been awake most of the day. Levet FaceTimed David with his daughter, Liza;

Levet's brother, Sonny, and David's sisters Bennie and Irene. David really engaged with Liza. She told her dad that she was on her journey, a New York University internship. Daddy's face reflected love and relief. "I was a bad girl, and now I'm a good girl," Liza said, and David's brows shot up. It was a funny and touching moment.

Levet and I are so excited about what has transpired today after weeks of David sleeping most of the time and offering monosyllabic responses to our requests to open his mouth, eat, swallow and so forth.

It's 4 p.m., and David is drifting off to sleep. He made a comment about someone "opening the gates." I asked him who was opening the gates, and he did not respond.

All the literature about the dying says patients rally before the storm clouds move in, and I wonder if today is the rally. I hope not. I pray for more good days.

There's an African American gentleman here of slight build whom everyone refers to as "Doc," I'm told that he once taught at Emory University. I'm told he's been a patient at OLPH for quite some time. I encountered him in the dayroom across the hall from David's room, and he said to me, "I'm trying to decide if I should go to Detroit, but I don't know if it's any better there." He's quite literate and reportedly taught Spanish at some time.

Here are some of the things that David said today that I don't want to forget: One of his sisters asked him how he felt, and David said, "When I'm tired, I lay down." When he FaceTimed with Lawrence, his dear friend joked with David and said, "I've got a blunt for you." David flashed a smile, almost as if to say, "I'd love to smoke a joint right about now." I saw David tear up from time to time. Levet insists that his father has an eye infection, but I would swear that I saw tears. In fact, I asked David directly, "Are you crying?" and he said, "Yes." And I believe him. My conclusion: David cried today, not a flood of weeping, just a stray tear here and there.

"Hot Wheels" is loudly suffering. He's crying out and making noises that indicate pain. It's been two days of this. I considered his noisiness, compared to David's quietness. Interesting how each person's journey reflects perhaps how each person is different in their pre-terminal-illness lives. David, for example, was not a noisy person before he got sick.

Thursday, Dec. 11, 2014
Our Lady of Perpetual Help Home

Arrived later than usual. Sadly, "Hot Wheels" died last night or very early this morning. Another man, a black man named Luke, is in the bed by the window so recently occupied by "Hot Wheels," who was on his feet and was even able to go to the bank in a cab just a few days ago. I have no idea how long "Hot Wheels" had been ill, what the nature of his illness was, or how long he had been at Our Lady, but he seemed to go downhill fast. Lord, have mercy on his soul. He was so loud at one point that David's eyes shot open as if to say, "What in the hell?"

It's dinner time, and I'm going to try to wake David to feed him. He wasn't hungry, so I took up my position in the chair beside his bed. Calls I've received so far today: Santa Wright, Christi Robinson, and my Chum club member Cheryl Tinker, all from Louisville. Vanessa Williams emailed. Levet called. Talked with Sadiqa Reynolds, my brilliant play daughter in Louisville, a good while last night.

Saturday, Dec. 13, 2014
Our Lady of Perpetual Help Home

David has been very quiet today even though Our Lady has had a lot of excitement. Students from Georgia Tech, including three from Italy, went to all the patient's rooms singing Christmas carols. David never woke up, but I enjoyed the music for him. The dayroom was decorated for the birthday celebration of another patient. The staff served punch, cake and Christmas cookies. The birthday boy got gifts. It was wonderful hearing the laughter of the children of his family.

Levet, Shanti and Aryanna visited. The caretakers got David into a recliner with wheels, and Levet took his dad outside to soak up the sun. David didn't open his eyes, but he seemed to enjoy the fresh air and the salsa music that Levet played on his iPhone. I figured the trip to the OLPH garden would knock David out. I was right. He's been asleep ever since.

I'm sitting here listening to Barbra Streisand's "Partners" and Kem's "Intimacy" albums. It's just before dinner, and things are quiet at Our Lady.

David's younger sister Irene called. I put the phone to David's ear. "I love you, too," he said.

I looked at David's face and his eyes, the windows to his soul, grew moist and red. He was crying softly. Tears streamed down his cheeks. Tears of grief? Maybe. Tears of love? Maybe. Tears of frustration? Maybe that he's talking, but we cannot understand. David's brain won't let him put it all together, and he seems very aware that he has no control.

Sunday, Dec. 14, 2014
Our Lady of Perpetual Help Home

Woke up at Gloria's house in Fairburn feeling "well slept." Thank you, God. Gloria left a note saying that she was going to pick up mail at the home of her son, Dr. Tony Pinder. (He is in Barcelona for work but still has a home in Georgia). He will fly back tomorrow to Boston, where he is a vice president at Emerson College. Tony is living his dream and making Gloria the proudest mother ever. It's 10 a.m. now, and soon I will get up, shower, dress, eat breakfast and then go to spend the rest of the day with David. He's my love — maybe my last — and I will hold on until God says it is over, and then I will have my memories — the good, the bad, the funny, the sad.

Gloria sat with me at Our Lady. David had very little to say other than a loud, "No!" when I asked if he wanted more dinner.

Eyes closed, he ate little and drank nothing on my watch. He puckered up for my kisses but made no eye contact. I didn't like the look of the splotches on his hands. Maybe he's allergic to something. By the time Gloria and I left him, David's eyes were closed, but I do believe that he was listening to the music that I played on the laptop. In my awful voice, I sang love songs to David anyhow. He was in no position to laugh at me or to complain. Gloria and I had dinner at Longhorn's, and by 10 p.m., I was in bed.

Tomorrow, I will repeat the cycle. Maybe David will have a good day by which I mean he may be more responsive. Whatever, God.

Monday, Dec. 15, 2014
Our Lady of Perpetual Help Home

David apparently was alert and conversant with OLPH staff and Levet but not so much with me. At one point, he actually seemed to be angry with me — and even seemed to be glaring at me. It was probably my imagination, and it was silly of me, but I went outside David's room and cried. It feels selfish of me to be thinking of how I feel as if David is himself. It's irrational because I know that David loves me.

Meanwhile, I do wish that Liza would come to Atlanta to see her dad even if it's just for a day. Maybe I'll suggest to Levet that he use some of his dad's money to get her a ticket, maybe for the train or the bus.

So much is happening in this world: Bill Cosby rape allegations; the Ferguson, Missouri, and Staten Island, New York, non-indictments of white cops who killed unarmed black men. Ordinarily I would have a lot to say about this, but it all seems so distant. Right now, my whole world is in this room with David. I can't use my outrage emotions for those issues when my own life is in upheaval, and I don't know what tomorrow will bring.

Tuesday, Dec. 16, 2014

Our Lady of Perpetual Help Home

David's eyes are open. He's talking, listening to music, making connections, answering questions, eating chocolate and, it seems, flirting with me. He's reaching out as if he is trying to touch my breasts. He got my attention with a whistle-like sound. When I turned toward him, he puckered up for a kiss. "Do you want anything?" I asked and David said, "Yeah, a soda." I put some Pepsi in a sippy cup. He held the cup for a while and then drank. He seemed to revel in those small moments of independence.

Dr. Read came as he does every Tuesday and Thursday. He observed David, listened to my report of it being a good day, then he moved on. "So long as he's comfortable," the doctor said. He offered no prognosis today. To be honest, comparatively, David has had a good several days.

When I got to Our Lady, David and his roommate, Luke, were being serenaded by a black church group. The singers gave each of them a bag of Christmas candy, as well as Christmas cards from each member of the group. After a while, David settled back into quietness. I sense his frustration that I can't understand what he's saying.

As my time to leave approached, I set David's cards up on his nightstand in front of the teddy bear that St. Nick had given him. "I'll see you tomorrow," I said, and David seemed surprised. "Isn't this my house?" he asked. When I responded, "No," he asked, "Well, whose house is this?"

"It's the nun's house," I said. (The sisters live on the other side of the building). "OK," he said. I felt incredibly sad. I hated to leave him. Oh, and for the second day, I noticed a tremor on David's right side.

I still hope that Liza will make it to Atlanta to see her dad, but every family is different. In any event, Levet's brother, Sonny, is supposed to come Friday to see David. I believe that David will love that.

Wednesday, Dec. 17, 2014
Our Lady of Perpetual Help Home

Today is David's 21st at Our Lady, and what a day it is. David was fairly alert and gave me much to smile about. I massaged his chest and asked if it felt good. He didn't say anything, but his face looked well pleased. Later, I was feeding David and asked if he wanted anything else. "No, Betty!" he replied in an unusually clear and loud voice.

Two women, one from Guatemala and the other from Colombia, visited the patients today. They were accompanied by several children. The women and the children seemed delighted that David also spoke Spanish. The children gave David a pair of socks, Christmas cookies, a homemade Christmas card with buttons and sang to him a few lines of "Feliz Navidad."

I played Latin music on the laptop for David, including the song "Muñeca" by Jimmy Sabater. "What does *muñeca* mean?" I asked, and David translated for me. "It means doll." David was listening intently to the music and at one point drummed on his food table with his good hand.

Finally, visiting hours were over. "I love you," I said, and David replied loud and clear, "I love you too, Moo Moo." He continues to astound me with his resilience. I would love it if he could be allowed to put his feet on the floor. He would love that.

Today, Christi Robinson, a friend from Louisville, LaVerne Vance from Maryland and my sorority sister Helen Swain from Louisville called.

Thursday, December 18, 2014
Our Lady of Perpetual Help Home

A quiet day for the most part. David didn't eat lunch but ate well for dinner — string beans, yams, a little turkey, nearly two cups of chocolate ice cream and a whole cup of apple juice. He's alert now after napping most of the afternoon. He was still awake, however, when an African American harpist, a retired teacher, she said, came through and played a couple of songs for David and Luke.

David is staring at nothing that I can see, and I'm wondering what he's seeing and thinking. The tremors are now showing up on both his hands.

It's 6:05 p.m., and Peter, a Kenyan male nurse, is cleaning David up and getting him settled in for the evening. These are wonderful people. God bless these gentle caregivers.

And in the news: President Obama announced normalization of U.S./Cuba relations yesterday, and everybody is talking about it.

Last night, Gloria and I did a lot of talking about David, about life, about sisters, about things that happened early in our lives that helped make us the women we are today. Her son, Tony, called from Boston and asked us to turn on the new TV show, "Sorority Sisters" on VH1, a reality show about nine African American women representing four black sororities. It is ratchet. Won't watch again. It was an unrealistic representation of black sorority life. The national organizations of the sororities applied pressure and got it taken off the air. Glo and I finally turned in about 1 a.m.

David's sisters Millie and Irene called today and so did my friends Mae Jackson, Marita Willis and Vanessa Williams. Had dinner at Big Daddy's soul food restaurant on Old National Highway with my old friend Rilea Arnett. When I had my TV show in Louisville, Rilea did the make-up for me and the guests and went out on some of the shoots that James "J.J." Jordan," the producer, set up. Rilea moved from Louisville to the ATL-area a few years ago. We called J.J. in Vegas where he's lived for the last several years. It was a fun reunion of old friends.

Friday, Dec. 19, 2014
Our Lady of Perpetual Help Home

Today was largely uneventful. David didn't talk much, but he did eat dinner — a slice of pepperoni pizza, chocolate cake — and drank a half glass of juice. Most memorable moment: David was being cleaned up — a diaper change — and repositioned in bed behind the curtain around his bed. I could only see David's face, and he could see me. I was stunned when he flashed a mischievous smile and stuck out his tongue toward me. Moments later, he fell fast asleep.

Saturday, Dec. 20, 2014
Our Lady of Perpetual Help Home

I arrived at Our Lady later than my usual, around 2:30 and with good reason: Aryanna's 10th birthday party at a roller-skating rink in Smyrna. Had a nice conversation with Shanti's mom and sister. Later, Aryanna, Levet and Sonny met me at Our Lady. David was never fully awake and didn't respond as he usually does when I ask for a kiss. I couldn't rouse him for dinner and was so concerned about the slight rattle in his breathing, the involuntary twitching on both sides of his body, and how he sometimes holds his good arm in the air for a long time. I asked Sister Mae to check him. She called his name loudly, and David opened his eyes but didn't speak. Sister Mae said, "This may be the change, but we'll see tomorrow. Every day is different." I was feeling uneasy. Sister Mae hugged me and said, "We'll see tomorrow."

I talked to Sadiqa from Louisville today; David's sister Irene, in New York; my NABJ friend Sidmel Estes, who was in Fairburn, and my god sister JoAnn in Philadelphia. My club, the Louisville Chapter of Chums Inc., called me from its annual Christmas party and sang a couple of Christmas carols to me.

Tuesday, Dec. 23, 2014
Our Lady of Perpetual Help Home

David got a manicure today, and his eyes were open when Santa Claus came to Our Lady, accompanied by the nuns wearing reindeer ears and ringing bells. Our Lady was buzzing with activity today with families and individuals coming through bearing gifts and glad tidings for David and the other patients. Some evenings it's especially difficult for me to leave David. I wonder what's going on behind his staring eyes and the hours of silence. What's he thinking? What's he wanting to say? Sometimes I feel as if I can sense him screaming from his body, "I want to get out. I want to walk again, be a man again and not wearing diapers and having to be changed like a baby." That's what I think, but God only knows. Meanwhile, I thank you, God, for peace and for this wonderful place, Our Lady, where my beloved is being treated so well and so compassionately.

Wednesday, Dec. 24, 2014
Christmas Eve
Our Lady of Perpetual Help Home

OLPH is unusually quiet today. Got here around 2 p.m. David is asleep or at least in an eyes-closed state. He looks so handsome lying there with that one arm reflexively raised in the air. We're planning a 6 p.m. FaceTime with his sisters, who will gather at Bennie's house for the call.

My haircut isn't like Virginia's (my regular stylist in Louisville). Should have known better than to let an unfamiliar hairdresser cut it. Bought a little wig that I probably won't wear. Anyhow, I'll try it.

Tomorrow, Christmas, I will come a little early to be with David and hang out later with Gloria and Georgeann. It's a contradiction, but this is my saddest Christmas and yet best Christmas ever. Perhaps, the best way to describe it is bittersweet.

Bitter because of David's condition. The cancerous tumors seem to have robbed him of emotion, outwardly laughing, crying and being empathetic. Still, who knows what David is feeling but simply can't articulate because his brain won't let him. Sweet because of the FaceTime David had with his sisters Bennie; Millie; and Irene; and his nieces, Bennie's daughter Caridad and Giga, his sister Cookie's daughter, and Caridad's girls. Levet, Shanti and Aryanna were on the call too. It was touching. The sisters would love to be near their big brother, but finances and health challenges make that impossible.

Sonny, Levet's older brother, who also lives in New York, was able to visit David over the weekend. The blessing is that the New York family is connecting with Levet and Aryanna.

Sweet, because as evening fell, the lights were turned down, and the Dominican Sisters of Hawthorne, the nuns who have operated Our Lady in Atlanta for 75 years, went from room-to-room carrying lighted candles and singing Christmas carols to the patients. In the darkened room, they gathered around David's and Luke's beds singing. It was beautiful and spiritual.

Tonight, I felt the true meaning of Christmas. God blessed David to be in this environment at this very important time in his life. I'll never forget this day. God bless the Dominican Sisters of Hawthorne.

Thursday, Dec. 25, 2014
Christmas Day
Our Lady of Perpetual Help Home

Breakfast and conversation with Gloria and then to OLPH to be with David. When I arrived, he was sitting in a recliner in the dayroom as his bed was being cleaned down to the mattress. David had a spoonful of pureed turkey and mashed potatoes, and that was enough. He did, however, eat a cup of ice cream, and he drank a whole can of Pepsi. Held the cup himself and sipped through a straw. At some point, he got annoyed with me when I kept trying to get him to eat. "No, Betty!" he said fairly loudly. I did get David to pose for a photo with me that I put on Facebook and texted to a few friends.

When I left Our Lady at 2:30, David was back in bed and asleep, and none too soon after several hours sitting propped up in the recliner. "I've got cramps," he said to me. He couldn't wait to get back in bed.

Got back to Gloria's in time for her annual Christmas dinner with some of her friends; her son, Tony; and his son, Mariano. Food was great. Then, I drove over to Georgeann's house in Riverdale. G had a full house with her friends and their children. My niece Muffy came too. I stayed a few hours and drove back to Gloria's in Fairburn. Tony, a Kappa Alpha Psi fraternity member, gifted me a beautiful pair of red leather gloves. His fraternity and my sorority both have crimson and cream as our official colors. I also received two candles from Bath & Body Works.

It was a long day, and old girl, that would be me, was ready for bed.

Saturday, Dec. 27, 2014
Our Lady of Perpetual Help Home

Breakfast with Gloria then off to be with David. He had visitors today. My friend Lynette and her husband, Tony McGriff. They stopped in on their way back to Louisville after spending the holidays in Georgia. David perked up during their visit. Later, on the phone with his sister Irene, he said, "I'm getting better." Irene was genuinely moved to hear her brother speak. I was moved too that David responded to my question, "Who loves you?" by pointing at me. He gave me lots of kisses. As I was leaving, I blew him a kiss, and he blew one back at me.

David's spoken words today:

"Where's my wallet?"

"Where's the elevator?"

"Who has the keys to the gate?"

Oh, and let me not forget that when Lynette and Tony were still there, I asked David if I was talking too much. He nodded his head to say, "Yes," and Lynette and I laughed.

Today's callers included some friends from Louisville, Clay Calloway, Clest Lanier and Marilyn Harrod; Jimmy Rollins from St. Louis; as well as my sister Debbie from New York; my niece Bernadette from South Georgia; and Levet.

Sunday, Dec. 28, 2014
Our Lady of Perpetual Help Home

My mother's best friend, Miss Theresa Stephens from New York and her daughters, Beverly and Lorraine, both of whom relocated to Metro ATL years ago, visited today. Mostly David slept and spoke very little. Gloria, Tony and his son, Mariano, went to see the movie, "Selma" today, and they loved it. Gloria said she wants to see it again with me. "You'll know a lot of the people," she said.

Treated myself to dinner at Ruby Tuesday. I had steak and lobster tail (tiny), but it was tasty. Read my book and contemplated many more dinners alone (again!). I'm missing David something fierce. Yes, he's a pain in the butt sometimes, but he's fun and I miss us talking about nothing.

Monday, Dec. 29, 2014
Our Lady of Perpetual Help Home

David was awake for most of my visit, but he spoke very little. "I wish you would talk to me," I said, and he said, "There's nothing to talk about." I kissed David a lot and played some of his favorite music. He closed his eyes and seemed to be enjoying Sarah Tavares singing in Portuguese immensely.

Sometimes, David stares at me intensely without blinking, and I feel that he's wordlessly trying to talk to me. He touches my face tenderly and kisses me just the same. The caretakers were changing David behind the curtain around his bed, and I peeked. David's eyes twinkled, and he puckered up a kiss. At the moment, I have a tummy ache and diarrhea. Nobody's going to change my diaper so I'm going to the bathroom.

Wednesday, Dec. 31, 2014
Our Lady of Perpetual Help Home

Yes, it's a *new year*, and by God's grace, David is still here and breathing. Never mind that he slept through the New Year's Eve celebration at Our Lady. He sat in the recliner in the party room downstairs and slept through the noise makers, the sparkling juice, the cake, the light hors d'oeuvres and the bingo games. David is undoubtedly in a different space.

Still, it was a wonderful celebration, yet another effort by the amazing nuns and staff to bring joy to people near the end of their lives and to their loved ones struggling to understand that our realities are about to change. Someone we love and who loves us, is on a journey that we won't be able to complete with them, though we well may meet again on the other side.

My sister Georgeann and a friend stopped in to see David. G put a New Year's hat on David's head. He really loves my sister, and I imagined that if he had the energy, they would have had a good laugh together.

(I did not make any entries in my journal for almost 10 days.)

Friday, Jan. 9, 2015
Our Lady of Perpetual Help Home (OLPH)

I had to go back to Louisville for the first few days of January to take care of some personal affairs. My soror Shorye Payne, who happened to be in Atlanta visiting, picked me up at Our Lady and drove me home. We talked about life and my situation during the six-hour drive.

Today, I got up at 5 a.m. and was out the door by 6. Donald Robinson, who entertained us at his home in Louisville and who visited David in the hospital in Louisville and at Our Lady in Atlanta, agreed to pick me up on his way to work and drop me off at the Mega Bus stop downtown for the ride back to Atlanta that day. I was emotional after not seeing David for a few days. My niece Tinisha aka "Muffy" and her beau, Ty, picked me up in Atlanta and drove me to Our Lady, where my car was parked. When I got back to Our Lady, David knew that I was there, and perhaps he had missed me. He's clearly getting weaker, but God's got him. He puckered up for a kiss, and when I laid my head on his chest, he embraced me with his good arm.

Saturday, Jan. 10, 2015
Our Lady of Perpetual Help Home

Staying with Levet and Shanti. I slept well, got showered and dressed. Said so long to the family and stopped at Publix to get a sandwich on the way to the expressway. Now, I'm sitting at David's bedside. He's weak, and he's eating and drinking less, but he's as handsome as ever.

I was sad to return and discover that David's roommate Luke had died. I really liked him and his family. Like David, Luke was mostly quiet. Also, like David, Luke loved sweets, and I'm glad that from time to time I gave him a helping hand. R.I.P. Luke. He's the third of David's roommates to pass since we arrived on Thanksgiving Eve.

Had a lovely conversation today with the chief administrator of Our Lady, Sister Damien. She comforted me, and when I commented that I didn't know how she and the other sisters can do this work, the constant coming and going, getting attached to patients and seeing them go. She looked at me and said, "We can do this work because we know where they are going." That's what allows them to celebrate the passing of each life they have touched, and I imagine hundreds of loved ones just like us have grieved even as our loved ones yet live.

God, thank you for the lessons I'm learning on this journey with David. Each day, I am reminded that he came back into my life to love me and to teach me.

David's got a new roommate, named Darryl. I loved that we've moved David's bed closer to the window. It's 4:50 p.m., and the setting sun is shining on David's face. He's a child of the sun and the ocean. I'm playing Danilo Pérez, a Panamanian pianist on my laptop and David's breathing peacefully, mouth slightly ajar.

Monday, Jan. 12, 2015
Our Lady of Perpetual Help Home

David is mostly silent now. Eyes rarely open. Not interested in eating or drinking. Tried to serve him Boost, but his mouth is tightly clenched, and the energy drink dribbled down his face. He no longer makes an attempt to remove the residue from his face.

When I arrived today, David had a second roommate, and the room feels a bit crowded. Darryl was behind his curtain all day and couldn't be heard over the very loud sound of his oxygen machine. The other gentleman is mobile and at one point began peeling off his clothes, so the aides closed his curtain, too. Gospel music is playing softly in the background. It's a pleasant hum. I kissed David repeatedly hoping to hear him say something, hoping he wakes up and talks coherently.

Give me some sign Papi Chulo, Don DaVid, Moodles, that you're still in there, even though your body is failing you.

Thursday, Jan. 15, 2015
Our Lady of Perpetual Help Home

Eventful day. Got here around 2:15 p.m. Interestingly, David is a bit more responsive. He didn't eat dinner, but he responded to Dr. Read's loud voice. His improved state may be due in part to his nephew Erin's visit. He seemed aware that Erin was here. Bravo. FaceTimed briefly with David's sister Irene. She was so happy to see her brother, and he responded to her, especially when she spoke to him in Spanish, using a phrase their mother often said, "Ay Bendito." Bendito means "blessed," but the phrase is equivalent to "Oh, Lord!" — expressing compassion or dismay.

It's 6 p.m., and David seems a bit restless. He's making guttural sounds and breathing loudly. His complexion looks beautiful.

Dr. Read said that he would be back to see David in a few days.

Perhaps overnight or early this morning, David's roommate Darryl died. By the time I arrived, Darryl's bed had been stripped. Darryl wasn't here long — maybe a week — but I did speak briefly with his nephew and a young lady who came to visit. Darryl asked them for water several times. Before they left, the young people promised Darryl that they would come to see him today. I'm sure now that they're glad that they didn't put off visiting the day before.

Now, just two people remain in the room, David and a man named Peter.

It's 6:05 p.m., and Sister Damien is offering evening prayers over the loud speaker.

I went to see "Selma" with Gloria yesterday before coming to see David. The movie was very good. Gloria who was not involved in the movement but knew I was, and so she wanted to know more. I explained that the movie was mostly about Dr. King's role in Selma and doesn't begin to tell the whole story. Of course, I'm not one who expects a movie to do everything. Movies offer just a slice. I suggested to Gloria that she would get a deeper understanding watching the documentary, "Eyes on the Prize."

Saturday, Jan. 17, 2015
My House
Louisville, Kentucky

I visited David very early this morning before heading back to Kentucky. Told David that I loved him and would be back Tuesday.

Alas, it was not to be.

I was back in Kentucky when David died at 2:15 p.m. David's death certificate, signed by Dr. Read and Sister Mae, attributed his immediate cause of death to "metastatic non-small cell lung cancer to the brain."

My Moodles gave up the ghost when no one was looking.

Chapter 18

Miss You - (Etta James)

Long before David became terminally ill, he told his family that he wanted to be cremated. His son shared the gist of one of those conversations with me:

"If I die, wait at least three days before you cremate me. Make sure that I'm good and dead."

And Levet said, "Like Jesus?"

And David said, "You never know."

And Levet said, "So, you want me to sit you in a cooler like cold cuts?"

Those two, father and son, often went back and forth with jokes and engaging in good-natured competitions. For example, which of the two was the best cook or whose coquito was the most authentic.

"You take shortcuts," Levet chided David. He didn't deny it, but the Louisville beneficiaries of David's Christmas coquito that he delivered in recycled liquor and wine bottles, didn't complain. Of course, they had no basis for comparison. One of my friends was in the habit, she told me, of stashing her coquito way in the back of her refrigerator. She didn't really want to share it with other family members. David did a lot of taste-testing during the preparation. His generous use of over-proof rum in his version of coquito turned an innocent-looking holiday drink into a knockout punch for the unprepared.

David and Levet's good-natured verbal jousting was, at times, right up there with, and I'm telling my age — Laurel and Hardy or the Three Stooges. Regrettably, they would never get to take their comedy show on the road. They really were a laugh riot.

Five days after David's passing, most of his ashes were interred in the memorial garden of Holy Spirit Catholic Church in Buckhead, just north of Atlanta. (The rest were to be scattered over the ocean in Puerto Rico.)

We stood single file: Levet; his wife, Shanti; their daughter, Aryanna; Shanti's mother, Robbie Dozier; Levet's mother, Juanita Cruz-Cataquet; my sister Georgeann Winston Eaddy; my cousin Gloria Pinder Jackson; David's dear friends Ibin Muhammad; Lawrence, and Pamela Roy; and me. The air was crisp during the 25 minutes or so it took for Father. Paul Burke to perform the Catholic Rite of Committal. Father Paul serves Holy Spirit Church and is also a chaplain of Our Lady of Perpetual Help Home.

Father Paul suggested burying David's ashes in the church's memorial garden, and Levet was very receptive. "I didn't want to keep my father's ashes in the house. I didn't want to sit my Dad up in a closet or up on the mantle," he said.

The interment ritual included no formal eulogy, but we eulogize David all the time in our prayers and with the stories we share about him. Whether funny, painful or poignant, the stories connect us and comfort us in David's absence.

That day in the memorial garden, I stood next to Levet. I was trembling so badly that for balance I held on to my sister's arm. I feared that I would collapse under the tonnage of my grief. I was so absorbed in my pain that I barely heard anything that Father Paul was saying. To be honest, that entire morning would be one big blur if not for the photographs that Levet's mother was kind enough to take using the iPad that David had given me.

I suspect that everyone in the memorial garden that morning was lost in their own thoughts about what we were witnessing and experiencing. I can imagine what everyone was thinking as I looked at Levet standing tall and holding with both hands the biodegradable green box that held his father's ashes.

Lawrence, Pam and Ibin, for example, could have been thinking about the joyous smile David flashed when they came to visit David at Shanti and Levet's house. David was conscious then but in the early stages of sinking into the mental fog that unfortunately would worsen in the weeks to come. On that day, what David couldn't put in words he said with his eyes. We were waiting for the ambulance to take David to the Tranquility hospice in Austell. When it pulled into the driveway Ibin and Lawrence didn't wait for the attendants. They each took a side and hoisted David upright in his hospital bed. David smiled the whole time. I captured that moment in a photograph.

And Aryanna? Maybe "baby girl," as David called her, was thinking about how much she was going to miss her grandpa or about how during his in-home hospice care, she was his faithful attendant, fetching him cookies, cupcakes, milk or whatever else her grandpa's sweet tooth was craving. While some youngsters are uncomfortable with sick people, Aryanna was tender toward the old man, and he lavished her with attention.

Shanti may have been contemplating how to comfort her husband as he grieved the loss of his amigo, his dad. It's not every woman who would have been comfortable turning her living room into her father-in-law's hospital room. Shanti did that and also played nurse at times, catering to David's needs and whims. She handled all of it with uncommon kindness and grace.

Perhaps Robbie, Shanti's mother, was recalling that one of David's last acts while he was still mobile was navigating the steps at Shanti and Levet's house in the wee hours to get her cake.

My sister Georgeann, besides worrying about me, could have been recalling the week that David stayed at her house while I was in New Orleans attending a National Association of Black Journalists' convention. David and Georgeann ate out every night the week that he was there, and David "Mr. Hotbox," kept her central air running full blast. Over one of their meals, David said to my sister, "Georgeanna, (he always pronounced her name with a Spanish inflection), I love your sister Betty but, you know, sometimes she talks so much that it blows my high." I howled when Georgeann reported that conversation.

And my cousin Gloria, bless her heart, could have been thinking about the loving care she extended to me when I stayed at her house off and on while David was at Our Lady. She cooked breakfast every day of my stays and prepared snack bags for me to take with me to the hospice. She washed and folded my clothes. And just as we did during those summers of our youth that I spent with her, her sister Judy, Uncle Joe and my godmother, Sarah, back in Philadelphia, Gloria waited up for me each night. She let me talk and cry about how helpless and frightened I was watching David slip away from me and this world.

And what about Juanita? What might Levet's mother have been thinking? Maybe about meeting and falling for David when she was a young woman and all the times that he disappointed her and their son. Yet, Juanita and her sister Margie visited David at Tranquility Hospice, and they were there when we dropped David off at Our Lady. Juanita is a stand-up woman for whom I have much respect. She came from New York to support their son, and though big David wasn't verbal, I read his face and body language as saying to the mother of his son, "I'm glad to see you. Thank you for coming." David told me that he had loved Juanita and that it broke his heart when she moved on with her life without him as a central figure.

Then there was Levet. That young man could have been having a million thoughts but perhaps none more sobering than that his father was gone, really gone, leaving behind no embalmed, suited up and made up corpse for him or anyone to touch and weep over. The Hardy to Levet's Laurel was gone never to call again with his familiar refrain, "*Yo loco!*"

Standing just a few feet away from the small open hole into which David's ashes were to be buried, Levet did not weep but later said, "The box was heavy."

The whole scene was heavy that morning, and things happened at the burial site and later that day, which, by our reckonings, or perhaps our deepest longings, appeared to be subtle messages from the outer limits that big Dave really was OK.

For example, I was momentarily distracted, and in a good way, by the laughter of children wafting through the window of a ground-floor classroom adjacent to the memorial garden. The happy sounds of the unseen little ones even as the ashes of an elder were being laid to rest in my mind symbolized the cycle of life: the beginning and the end.

After David's ashes were buried, most of us, joined then by my niece Tinisha and Ty, regrouped at Shanti and Levet's house for a repast. During the meal, Levet, Georgeann and Gloria talked about hearing a rooster crowing throughout the committal ceremony. It was very loud and insistent, they said. I must have been way off in space because I didn't hear the barnyard fowl. "Come on, y'all," I challenged. I couldn't imagine for a second anyone in Buckhead, one of the wealthiest communities in America, keeping chickens in the grand backyards of their mansions. Then again, wealthy people do all sorts of things for no other reason than that they can. The symbolism of the crowing rooster while we were bidding adieu to David had a special meaning, simply because when David was a youngster, his father called him "Rooster" because of the five youngest Rivera kids still living at home, David was the oldest and the only boy. So, when the elder David was away at sea, young David was effectively a rooster among the hens. He was the protector of his mother and younger sisters.

Millie, David's youngest sister, tells another rooster story. She said that family lore has it that friends of her parents showed up one day very agitated, alleging that David was making moves on their daughter. After the girl's parents made their case, David's mom rose up in defense of her son. She reminded the girl's parents that the situation was a two-way street and said, "I'll keep my rooster away from your hen, but you make sure to keep your hen away from my rooster. Remember, it's your hen who lays the eggs."

The crowing rooster wasn't the only odd occurrence the day that we committed David's ashes to the earth. After the repast, the Rivera household was quiet, when Shanti spied a yellow cardinal sitting on a post in their backyard. It was an unusual sighting. The bird sat for so long that she called Levet over to take a look. After a long while, the yellow cardinal flew away. Now, red cardinals are common, but yellow cardinals not so much. That being so, Shanti searched the internet to find out if the yellow cardinal symbolized anything special. And it did. One entry said that, "If a yellow bird is seen flying, it signifies that you will gain your freedom." The inference, of course, was that after a long struggle, her father-in-law was free. He had flown away, hopefully to paradise.

Of all the things that occurred toward the end of David's life, none strikes me as more meaningful and profound than the vision that David had while in hospice care at Levet and Shanti's house. David was sitting high up in his hospital bed when he looked at Levet and then down at an empty space and asked, "Who is that little boy standing next to you? He looks just like you." It could be that David was seeing himself with Levet when he was a little boy. At that stage of David's cancer journey, it wasn't unusual for him to hallucinate, or to put it another way, to dream out loud. So, we didn't attach great significance to David seeing an imaginary boy, but then in late September 2016, a curious thing happened.

Shanti was experiencing back pains severe enough that Levet took her to urgent care to be checked out. Tests confirmed that Shanti was having back pains because she was pregnant, and not just a little pregnant either. The baby was due in December. Shanti and Levet weren't planning for a second child. They believed that they had one, Aryanna, and that they were done. On December 19, 2016, Aryanna's 12th birthday, a baby boy was born. They named him David Johnathan Rivera.

"God works in mysterious ways," my mother often said, and I've found that to be true in my reconnecting with David after not seeing him in almost half a century, falling in love with him and traveling with him on his last earthly journey. It was quite a ride. David, the man, and his journey opened my heart and laid bare my soul. Loving and living with David taught me life lessons that I didn't know that I needed to learn and affirmed the wisdom of the elders.

One can argue, of course, that the symbolism of the rooster crowing; the yellow cardinal sighting; the laughter of the unseen children that I heard while standing in the memorial garden; and the birth of the baby boy were pure coincidences. Or, that in our grief, all of us were struggling to find meaning for David's life and ultimately peace in the wake of his death. But I believe in God's power, mercy and grace, and so I believe in miracles.

Amen.

Farewell my Love in the memorial garden of Holy Spirit Catholic Church in Buckhead

Farewell #2

A quiet space to meditate: The chapel at David's hospice.

Acknowledgements

First, I acknowledge God, whose voice instructed me to tell somebody about how (S)He kept David and kept me before, during and after David's cancer diagnosis and subsequent death in 2015.

I wrote on and off for months and eventually shared my rough musings with a few friends, including Audrey Edwards, an amazing writer and former editor at Essence and other magazines. She read several pages and gently said, "Now, you have to start writing." I appreciated Audrey's critique that I had more work to do. When I had a second draft, I turned to Angela Dodson, writer, editor and founder of "Editors On Call." Angela connected me with Janine Covenay, a freelance editor. Janine's probing questions, observations and suggestions caused me to dig deeper. I was still so emotionally raw that I stopped writing for a long while. The devil was busy and had me thinking that if I finished the book David would go away, and I wasn't ready to let him go.

Many friends knew that writing the book was part of my grieving process and they encouraged me to take one step at a time. God Bless you Sadiqa Reynolds, Gail Strange, Nadia Fischer, Everett Todd, LaVerne Vance, Ken Foree, Michelle Tyrene Johnson and Audwin Helton. Thank you, Hannah L. Drake for hooking me up with Julia A. Royston, my publisher. Julia, Angela and Diane Hawkins believed in my project and dragged me to finish line.

I would have drowned in my grief if not for the love and constant encouragement of Vanessa Williams; DeWayne Wickham; Dr. Sheila & Rodney Brooks; Jackie Jones; the Louisville Alumnae Chapter of Delta Sigma Theta Inc.; the Louisville chapter of Chums Inc.; and the Zora Neale Hurston Readers' Circle. Also, Joe & Sherrie Lyons; Mario & Beverly Johnson; Chuck & Clest Lanier; Donald & Christi Robinson and Rod & Angie Strickland.

Fran Hyman Price, my ride-or-die friend since 10th grade, and Mae Jackson cried with me over the phone and then turned around and made me laugh.

My sisters, Deborah Winston Blakes and Georgeann Winston Eaddy; nephews Darnell George Winston (Tamika Scott) and Roman Larry Phillips; my nieces Bernadette Eaddy Cooper (Kenneth) and Tinisha Eaddy; my great nephews Dayvon and Dorian; great nieces Destinee, Madiison, Armani, Oshun and Taniyah; my Godsister JoAnn Newkirk Wilkins (Joseph); and my cousins, always give me unconditional love and support. In the immortal words of Prince, I love you each of you with *"1,000 X's and O's."*

My faith and my spiritual life are well tended to by Dr. Kevin W. Cosby, senior pastor of St. Stephen Baptist Church and Rev. Geneva Nelson, able shepherd of the Christian Education Department and leader of the Coffee, Cafe and Christ Sunday School class. Much love to Rev. Dianne Brown, former associate pastor, who prayed with David and I throughout the journey and presided at David's memorial service. Thank you Margie Duvall, Soror Yolanda Buford-Demaree for helping me to plan the memorial.

To David's family: thank you for loving me and for sharing your father, brother, uncle and grandfather. I pray that I have done justice to the man that he was. He was imperfect for sure, but David was a good man at heart and he was the right man for me at the right time in our lives.

Finally, to the readers: If you feel so moved, in honor of David's memory and the memory of those close to you who are battling or have succumbed to cancer, please consider sending a contribution to Our Lady of Perpetual Help Home, 760 Pollard Blvd. SW, Atlanta, Georgia 30315. The home provides compassionate hospice care at no cost to patients or their families and relies solely on contributions.

Betty Winston Baye'

Journalist and motivational speaker, Betty Winston Baye, is author of "Blackbird" (August Press) and "The Africans" (Banbury/Dell). She's been published in *Louisville*, *Essence* and other magazines and has been featured in several books, including "Children of the Dream: The Psychology of Black Success" (Audrey Edwards and Dr. Craig Polite); "Work Sister Work: How Black Women Can Get Ahead in Today's Business Environment;" (Cydney Shields & Leslie Shields); and "Kentucky Women: Two Centuries of Indomitable Spirit and Vision" (Eugenia K. Potter). She contributed to the anthology "Thinking Black: Some of America's Best Black Columnists Speak Their Mind" (DeWayne Wickham, editor).

Betty is researcher/interviewer for the University of Kentucky's Civil Rights Hall of Fame Oral History Project and co-chair of the University of Louisville's Black Family Conference. She was an adjunct lecturer at Hunter College and Bellarmine University

She's a former reporter, editorial writer and columnist for *The Courier-Journal* (Louisville, KY) and previously a reporter for *The Daily Argus* (Mount Vernon, NY).

She holds a master's degree from Columbia University's Graduate School of Journalism and bachelor's degree from Hunter College, City University of New York. She was a Nieman Fellow at Harvard University in 1990-91. In 2013, Betty was inducted into the National Association of Black Journalists' Hall of Fame, and in 2016, HBCU Simmons College of Kentucky awarded Betty an honorary doctorate of humanities.

Betty is a past vice president and regional director of the National Association of Black Journalists. She founded the Zora Neale Hurston Readers' Circle in 1999. Other memberships include the Black Alumni Network of Columbia University's Graduate School of Journalism; Delta Sigma Theta Sorority Inc.; the Louisville Chapter of Chums Inc.; and St. Stephen Baptist Church.

For more information and booking, visit http://www.bettybaye.com or email bbaye2482@gmail.com.

Made in the
USA
Lexington, KY